Presenting to Engage

The secrets of effective presentations

Richard C Smith

Contents

Introduction

Communication has always been of supreme importance in business. Good communication with customers and colleagues leads to successful businesses and contributes to healthy sales, while poor internal and external communications are well known to have a negative impact on the bottom line. Now, technology has spawned a new genre, that of the slide-driven presentation. These have become the standard for everything from large product launches to job interviews, from lectures to meetings. Delivering presentations has become an activity that any middle or senior manager has to master in order to be fully successful. Increasingly, business leaders understand that the way an organisation presents itself has a tangible impact on their financial success. This is particularly evident in the technology sector.

Unsurprisingly, most people will have had to sit through some poor presentations during their career. Most people presenting have never had any training or guidance in how to present to an audience, and often make it worse for themselves by using presentation software poorly. In a business situation, poor presentational skills can adversely affect promotion prospects; they can cause lost sales and damage credibility and reputation of individuals and the organisation.

In this book, I will tell you the secrets that effective presenters use to interest and engage an audience of five or five hundred. I will divulge the golden rules of presenting to an audience, and tackle a few sins along the way. Since technology is such a huge part of our lives, I will show you how the technological tools that we have can be used to create engagement and the uses to avoid that will damage your credibility with your audience. In keeping this book concise, I hope to concentrate on the practical help that will bring you both quick wins and long term success in your presentations. This is a handbook on how to engage an audience and deliver presentations that are effective in their aims.

I have been presenting to others for over twenty years. I started my career as a secondary school teacher; this can be a harsh environment in which to learn how to engage a critical audience! Subsequently in my career, I left the classroom and found myself presenting to business professionals, senior leaders in local government, consultants and education professionals. I have worked with groups of three or four people, up to large audiences of several hundred. I have delivered literally hundreds of presentations in a business setting; many went well, some went poorly. It is this wealth of practical experience, along with the pedagogy gained from working in education, which I am now bringing to you in this book.

Presenting is a professional skill, and as such can be refined and improved. Whether you consider yourself a natural presenter or not, you will find plenty here to help you improve your effectiveness with audiences. I wish you good luck in your work presenting to others.

Richard Smith.

"It's all about you"

Let's get something straight right from the start. When you present, the focus of attention for most of the people most of the time is you. There may be some amazing technology available; there may be an exciting new product or service; you may have all sorts of multimedia at your disposal. None of that will save you if you present yourself poorly or fail to make a connection with your audience. So the basic building block of any presentation is the relationship that you build with the audience, and that starts with how *you* are.

There is a lot of erroneous advice spoken and written about presenting. Often, when the phrase *public speaking* is used, the advice can be out of date and miss the mark for business presentation scenarios. Unless you are presenting in a church or incredibly large and echo-filled venue, what you initially think about speaking to an audience may not be true. At this point, any vicars reading will be tempted to stop, but please persevere anyway!

So if you are the focus of your audience, it follows that the people sitting in the audience need to be your main focus. Now that might sound obvious and patronising, but how many presentations have you been to where the content was so important to the presenter that he or she almost ignored the audience, and there may as well have been shop dummies on the seats? For me, I've been to quite a few. Perhaps I've been unlucky!

Effective presenters start by knowing their audience. Not personally (but great if you do), but a few basics. Why have they come? Were they sent, or did they choose to attend? How familiar are they already with the content? What level are they in their organisation? I would suggest that knowing the answers to these questions is a basic requirement needed for planning an effective session. How you get to find out the answers will vary depending on the circumstances in which you have been asked to speak. If you are organising the event, or have influence over the organisation of it, then you should try to collect some basic information from participants as they sign up, if they are unknown to you. This is much easier if you are presenting to co-workers, although this can have different pitfalls, as we will see later.

By knowing the audience, even in a superficial way, we can change what we do to suit them. This is an incredibly important aspect that effective presenters do, often without realising it. No two presentations should be the same. Yes, I really mean it! The problem with presentations that are delivered to different groups in exactly the same way is that the audience are not exactly the same, and this usually means that the content has become more important than the people. That's a bad thing!

Always remember that the most important aspect of the whole presentation is the audience, the people in the room. A presentation should be influencing them in some way, usually to change behaviour. Even information delivery will have some higher, ulterior motive. If the presentation is not trying to influence them in any way, then a presentation is probably not the most suitable delivery mechanism. It will be dealing with how to influence and engage your audience later in the book.

Another issue to tackle straight away is that which you will hear from some people when faced with delivering a presentation – "I'm not a natural presenter". It is true that some people seem to have an aptitude for speaking to an audience and engaging with them, in the same way that Stephen Hawking has an aptitude for physics, or J.K. Rowling has an aptitude for storytelling. However, this does not mean that there is nothing that can be learnt about presenting, or that you cannot improve your skills. While we may not all be able to be as amusing or erudite as Stephen Fry, we can still give a good and effective presentation. Many activities in life are ones that we do not have a natural aptitude for, but we build an acceptable level of competency through practice and professional development. [This seems to be particularly true in the case of management, and this is surely the premise of the multitude of management training courses.] So if you feel that presenting is not something that you find easy, you will find many others who feel the same but who have become successful at it. Don't let that become an excuse for opting out of presenting. The purpose of this book is to encourage everyone to develop and improve their skills when presenting to an audience.

I will get into the specifics later, but just to get us going at the start, there are a few things that you can do to make your life easier when presenting, and ensure that you are as comfortable as possible. Here's a quick check list:

- Whatever the dress code, ensure that your clothes are as comfortable as possible. For men wearing shirts and ties, avoid shirts with tight collars.
- You will want to choose shoes that are comfortable, as there may be a lot of standing and walking.
- If you need spectacles to see the audience, wear them. As we will see later, effective presenters pick up on the body language and non-verbal cues of the audience members, so you need to be able to see them clearly.
- Check that there will be a glass of water if you need it.
- Double check how long you are speaking for, and if there are any breaks scheduled (both within your part and before or after).
- Have sight of a clock or watch. It is quite unprofessional when presentations overrun excessively, so you need to be able to keep a check on the time easily and without drawing attention to it.

If you are to feel at ease and give a good presentation, you will need to be knowledgeable about what you are presenting. While this may sound obvious, there are times in business where you may find yourself suddenly being asked to present on a topic in which you have limited knowledge and expertise. One response to this (and the one most likely to enhance your promotion prospects) is to research the content and become an expert. If this is not possible, and if you can get out of such things, you should do so. It is *your* credibility that is on the line if your end up looking uncomfortable or out of your depth. Presenters who are experts and have good understanding of the subject matter add extra content and value almost without realising. Those quick asides, odd details here and there, all make for an informative and more engaging experience.

Finally, the most important point is to "be yourself". I have attended some presentations where the presenter was trying to put on a bit of an act. If you do this, you may get away with it, particularly with larger audiences. But at some point you will be found out, especially when the audience is smaller or the content is more specialised.

It is perfectly possible to accentuate the positive aspects of your personality that are suited to presenting and suppress those that have a negative effect. But presenting is not acting, although it may share some common features. People are there to hear *you*, not a persona. The other problem is that unless you are an experienced actor, trying to be something that you are not is stressful and can be uncomfortable. All successful presenters do as much as they can to be at ease during the presentation (even if they get nervous beforehand). Please don't misunderstand me; there are useful techniques that actors use that will also be of use when presenting to an audience. The key difference is that you are not taking on another character. I am always suspicious when "resting" actors offer training in presentations for business. I often speculate as to how much practical experience they have of being themselves with an audience, and indeed how much experience they have of business presentations in general.

As you read on, remember that presenting is an art rather than a science, but knowing a bit of science can help. What I do not think you need to do is use a recipe for each presentation. There is a temptation in modern business to systemise everything, in order to gain consistency and facilitate quality control. I acknowledge that this can be effective in many situations. The problem with trying to do this with a business presentation is that it is an essentially creative task. We can try to quantify the stages in the process of preparing and delivering a presentation, or develop a methodology to use. Indeed, a quick trawl of the internet will bring up plenty of scientific-looking methods and detailed diagrams. If this sort of thing helps you, then that is fine. However, I take the view that variety can be good, and the needs and expectations of the audience are the most important thing. As your audience and the context change, so should your presenting; I hope this book reflects that reality.

The science bit

Well to be fair, I'm not going to throw too much science your way in this chapter. What I will do is give you some insight into your audience. Knowing how people learn and what engages them is the first step to effective presentation.

I am going to give you a quick summary of one of the main theories about how people learn. You may be already thinking that this is not a classroom, so what relevance does it have. The main purpose of any presentation is to influence the audience members. That might be simply to know about some new information and act on it, or it might be about changing behaviours. It could be about influencing them to buy a new or different product, but influencing them is a common strand. To do that, they will need to have some new information, and then to understand what that means for them. This is the same process that we use when we learn, even if the outcomes may look different. If we are to successfully influence and change behaviours, then the people in the audience will need to understand and internalise what they are seeing and hearing.

I must also give a bit of a health warning over theories of learning in general. A 2004 literature review looked at 71 different theories, including the one that I will expand upon later. For most of them, the authors concluded that there had been inadequate validation through independent research. I prefer to consider what follows as a model of how people learn and take in information, which is in fact how it was initially presented by the authors. A model differs from a theory in that a model does not necessarily claim to represent an underlying truth that can be universally applied, but to represent a framework that works well in certain circumstances. The line of thought that "there are so many theories and they cannot all be right" is not so important if we consider the so-called "theories of learning" to be in fact models, which allow us to enable learning more effectively.

A popular model of learning that I think matches my experiences over the last twenty years was written about in the paper Learning and Teaching Styles (Felder & Silverman, 1998). Reassuringly, the authors talk about it as a model. It says that there are three main styles of delivering content that enables people to learn. They are auditory (providing information through speaking), visual (providing information through images and writing), and kinaesthetic (providing information through practical tasks and activity). Most activities that are designed to influence or impart knowledge can have the elements for each of the three styles readily identified. As recipients of teaching or presenting, we respond to all three.

The significant point of this particular theory is that different people have different preferences in respect of the three learning styles. For example, some people may respond best to being told things, and clearly they would prefer an auditory style. However, others find it easier to learn when information is presented visually, with a series of written statements or some images. There are some people who take all this a little too far. They talk about "visual learners", as if those people only learn through visual stimuli. Of course, this is not entirely true. Other styles will still have an effect, but perhaps not as great. It is probably true to say, however, that most people have a preferred learning style out of the three.

There is a small industry that has grown up of providing questionnaires that determine the balance of preference for a person, and books on this subject. I will save you the time and effort by distilling the key points here and putting my own interpretation on them based on my experiences as a presenter.

As any group is likely to contain a mix of people with different preferred learning styles, it means that as a presenter we should not rely on any single one for all of the content. This means that the presenter who proclaims (usually a little smugly) that they are doing without slides and visual stimuli from a computer is doing just as big a disservice to some members of the audience as the presenter who puts everything on slides and says very little. Clearly, a presentation with a balance and variety of styles will engage the most members of the audience. In a business presentation setting, it may be harder to use kinaesthetic styles. However, we may still be able to provide some interactivity, and I come to this in greater detail in a later chapter.

It is also true that the amount of information retained by people depends on the mode of delivery, and there are some general conclusions that seem to be true for most people. Broadly, the more active the mode of delivery, the more information is retained. Simply hearing information leads to the lowest retention, while writing does slightly better, doing an activity is better still, and the best is teaching someone else about the topic. This is why school students are often asked to make notes during their learning, as the act of doing so will cause more of the information to be retained than if they had simply listened to the teacher. Clearly, in a normal business presentation setting, we may be limited in what we can ask audience members to do, but engaging them in some way will lead to greater retention of the subject matter.

Planning your pitch

The first stage in any presentation is planning what you are going to do. This procedure will be similar, whether it is a one-off event or a session that you will deliver many times. Even if you are provided with some content to deliver, there is still some basic planning that you will need to do. What I am about to say may seem obvious, but I have attended presentations where these points had clearly not been addressed.

- What is the overall purpose of the presentation?
- What outcomes are you expecting or hoping for?
- What is the audience likely to know already?

I would suggest that if you cannot answer any one of the questions above with ease, then there is some basic work to be done. It is unlikely that a presentation can be effective without the answers to these questions being known and understood by the presenter. These key points need to be in the back of your mind throughout the planning process, and every part of the presentation should be addressing one of these.

The next stage will be the setting out of the key ideas and messages that you need to get across during the presentation. Clearly, if you are presenting for a couple of hours, you will have the opportunity to say more than if you have a thirty minute slot, but there will usually be two or three key pieces of information or themes. The golden rule is to go for less and do each one better. If there are too many points or too much information to get through, presentations can become rushed. More importantly, over-busy presentations are easier for attendees to derail. If there are too many key points, then when you take questions you end up flitting around the content and the overall messages become confused or unclear. If there are fewer key messages, then even input from awkward attendees can be brought back to one of them.

At this stage, you may also want to consider the form that information takes. If there is a lot of information to elaborate on or to exemplify one of your key messages, then that should be given to attendees in the form of a hand-out or booklet. The same is true of anything that attendees may want to refer to later. As we will see later, any slides shown should be fairly minimal in terms of information that they display. So decide at this stage what the "take away stuff" is and therefore should be produced as printed material, and what is presentation content. Of course, there may be some content that is both.

As a broad rule, give the detail as hand-out and keep the key messages and broad thinking as presentation and slide content.

I am going to assume that when it comes to what content to include, and how to say what you want to say, you are the expert. Each industry has its own vocabulary, common conventions and ways of working. As I concentrate on the aspects of presentation technique, you should also be considering exactly what you will be saying. If you have to present on a topic, then presumably someone considers you to be an expert on it, or at least someone worth listening to. Therefore, trust your ideas on the subject matter and what key messages to include.

Before you start considering the slides you are going to use (and I am assuming that there will be some visual stimulus for the audience), you need to think about the overall structure. Rather like a good book, a presentation needs a beginning, middle, and an ending. Put another way, and to quote from an unknown source, start by telling them what you are going to say, then say it, and then tell them what you said. It is one of those clichés that actually works!

You should start by setting out your stall, so to speak. People generally like to know what they are going to be doing, so the start of any presentation should be fairly pacey, and provide the answers to these audience questions:

- Why am I here?
- What is the presentation about?
- What is the structure of the presentation?
- What will I know or understand afterwards that I did not know before?

Having the answers in your opening will do something very important. Your presentation should not be a "magical mystery tour" of content. While suspense is a tool that you can use to good effect at times, the audience should not be wondering where the presentation is going. Having a clear set of objectives and outcomes will help your audience understand why you (and they) are there and the benefit that they will derive from the session. Establishing the benefit is an important feature of an opening. It is quite common in presentations that are not focused on selling a product for the presenter to omit to "sell" the content. Your first job as a presenter is to affirm that the audience members have made the right decision in attending. This performs an important task, which is getting the audience on your side as early as possible.

So as you plan your opening, ensure that there are clear objectives (what the presentation is setting out to do) and clear outcomes (what the result of the presentation is). Clearly, presentations in some situations will not fit quite as neatly into this model, but it is still a good set of principles to try to work to. Having clarity with these points in the opening will also mitigate the attitude that some attendees will have of "this has nothing to do with me". This can be a particular issue where the audience contains many people who have been sent by their company, rather than chosen to attend themselves.

The opening is also your first opportunity to manage the expectations that attendees have about your presentation. In some respects, you could argue that the success or failure of a presentation is down entirely as to whether the expectations of the audience were met. This is why it is important to know and understand what your audience expects from you and your session when you are in the planning stage. If possible, make reference to any shared expectations during the opening. Expectations are often set in the pre-presentation material, such as advertising flyers or web pages. If you have control over such things (and sometimes you do not), you should try to ensure that materials set appropriate and realistic expectations. They should be expectations that you can meet and exceed.

One reason I have seen some presentations fail, and the audience become increasingly restless, is when expectations have been set far too high. In my work, one presenting task that I had to do frequently was to introduce a revised or new policy to managers. They were then expected to implement it in their own department. This is not an uncommon scenario in large organisations. Therefore, the presentations' objectives were typically framed around understanding the principles underlying the new policy and then covering the key non-negotiable elements. It would then move on from this to planning for a local implementation. However, some managers would come with the expectation of simply being given a list of jobs to do. In this situation, it should have been clear that a single solution or implementation was not appropriate for everyone, but this mismatch in expectations between presenters and (some) audience members inevitably led those attendees to be dissatisfied overall with the session. The unreasonable expectations had unfortunately been established prior to the session. However, a well-judged opening was often able to address this; explaining not only what was going to be done, but also why, could be used to attempt to modify the expectations of some attendees.

Starter activity

In some presentations, it is not appropriate for attendees to have much activity. However, some element of activity will often have a positive impact on the engagement of the audience. Part of your initial planning will involve deciding how active or passive the audience is going to be. If your presentation is short, but you have much information to get through, you may opt for little or no activity. The amount will also depend on the size of the audience and the layout of the room in which you will be presenting. It is a common misconception to assume that lots of activity is good, and no activity is bad. I'm going to introduce a golden rule here:

"All things in moderation."

Too much activity can be as bad as too little. There is no hard and fast rule, as the optimum amount will depend upon the presentation duration, purpose, audience size, audience expectations, etc. You should also avoid activities for their own sake. Everything in your presentation should have a clear purpose, preferably one that attendees can understand.

You also need to tap in to the expectations of the audience. In a large presentation, there may be an expectation that the experience is fairly passive. I have found that starter activities work best in smaller settings, where they may also work as an icebreaker. They should be relevant and contribute to the outcomes of the session. Beware of inadvertently trivialising the whole presentation right at the start.

A short starter activity can be useful to quickly engage the audience and also provide you with some useful feedback. When I have done starter activities, I try to keep them to five minutes or so, ten minutes as a maximum. I usually announce their purpose to the audience; of getting some initial feedback from them, or finding something out from them. Of course, it also has the effect of getting a bit of energy in the audience.

As to what your starter activity could be, there are many possibilities. Some that have worked well for me are:

- Quickly jot down three questions that you have about X.
- How many examples of X can you think of? You have thirty seconds.
- Ask two or three quick quiz-style questions on the presentation's subject, ensuring that most attendees will have some level of success.
- What do you already know about X, and think of one key thing that you would like to know.

Another good starter activity is getting some quick feedback using an audience response system. I will deal with this later in the chapter on interactivity, as such systems have their own benefits and challenges.

If you will be taking feedback, think how this will work. In order to be short and sharp, it is unlikely that you would have time (or want) to take feedback from everyone, so make it clear beforehand that you will take one or two quick points of feedback. Of course, if you have done something with an element of quizzing, you could simply have a show of hands as to who got all the questions correct, or who had the most examples of X written down.

Whatever you decide to do as a starter activity, make sure that it has a clear purpose, ensure that this purpose is communicated to the audience, and ensure that it is related in some way to the theme of the presentation as a whole.

The opening part of your presentation is very important when it comes to setting the tone of the session. The reality is that much of your audience will come to a conclusion about how good the session will be, based on the first couple of minutes, and possibly even based on what happens beforehand. A clear, professional start is essential.

If you have more than one person who will be presenting, resist the temptation to have too many changes of presenter. Certainly stick to one person for the opening section. For the reason stated in the paragraph above, you should put a strong presenter on first.

The main section

When it comes to the middle section of the presentation, this will be the main part of the session, both in terms of time and of content. It is very tempting to plan this part in terms of the slides that you think you will use. Resist this, and start with an outline of the sections that you want, and then flesh out each section. Remember the point that I made earlier about background material. This is a good opportunity to determine what should be provided in hard copy for attendees.

As you plan, imagine that you are telling a story, so the parts need to be linked and should follow on logically. At this point, you may also want to consider when and how to deal with questions from the audience. I will deal with this in the chapter on interaction, as there is plenty that needs to be said about it.

The content of the main part of a presentation often falls into one of several categories. It can be about selling (a product or an idea), providing an update of information, or a mix of the two. There are countless books written about selling and sales technique. I am not going to try to cover that ground, but there are some observations that I would make about typical sales presentations.

Some sales pitches fail because they try to put too much information into the presentation rather than in take-away material. They miss the human element of the product, in other words they tell me why it is a great product rather than why I need it. There are thousands of excellent products being sold, none of which I need! Also, announcing and selling a product to a group of people is a different proposition from selling to a single person. When people are in a group, there are group dynamics at play. Remember to plan for a call to action and make the unique selling points abundantly clear. What might be obvious to you may not be obvious to your audience.

As you plan out what you will say and do, you may go through two or three iterations, fleshing out the content at each stage. As you work towards the main part of the presentation, you are aiming to get to a point where all the key things you will say are written down somewhere as bullet points.

At this stage, perhaps I should lay my cards on the table as regards writing a script. For most business presentations, you should not write a word-for-word script that you try to learn. The reason why is obvious when you see people on the TV programme "Dragons' Den" trying to recite a script under pressure. They often fluff their lines, this makes them even more nervous, and they struggle to proceed with the pitch. Professional actors spend weeks rehearsing their lines. Most presenters in a business environment do not have that time. Also, as I have mentioned earlier, what you say may change depending on audience reaction and body language. It is not like a play, where it is supposed to be the same every night. If you have the benefit of an autocue, then by all means write a script. However, the vast majority of business presentations do not. It is also a fact of presentational life that audiences often do not like to feel that they are simply getting a script delivered to them. It is as if the audience came expecting a more personal touch, and are disappointed if they do not get it.

Most effective presenters that I have encountered use a series of bullet points. After all, if you are knowledgeable about the subject of the presentation, you should have already internalised the detail. The written bullet points are an *aide memoire*. For the moment, we will not worry about how you will access these notes during the presentation.

In my opinion, this planning stage is much easier when you use IT to help you. I have to confess that I use a mixture of IT and paper-based methods. The initial setting out of ideas I may do on paper. But I quickly move to a word processor or presentation software application so that I can edit easily, and more importantly, move sections of the draft presentation around.

The closing

All presentations need some sort of closing section. The conventional wisdom will point to some sort of summary of the main points, and I concur with this. You should also ask yourself what you want people to do as a result of the presentation. If it is to buy a product, include some call to action. If it is influencing them to change behaviour, reinforce the change (and the benefits). I would argue that all presentations should seek to change something, even if they may appear purely informational. Otherwise, what was the point of doing it? Also, there is a difference between simply repeating a few phrases and summarising points. Think of how you can get the key messages across in a different way than you tried earlier. Can you use different vocabulary? Can you use images or diagrams instead of speech, or vice versa?

The constant problem with a clearly demarcated closing section is that there may be some attendees who feel that they have heard everything and do not want to stay just to hear the same things again. I have been to numerous presentations where the odd few try to sneak out ten minutes before the end. Therefore, the challenge is to summarise and wrap up, but add something new. It is easy for the closing section to be the weakest of the presentation, particularly as you may be fatigued at the end. So keep something for the end, something that people will want to hear.

One device used by presenters like Steve Jobs is to have some content that is unexpected but exciting at the end. It is the "but one more thing" moment. Just when the audience thinks it is all over, there is a big announcement with a wow factor. Clearly, this is not going to be an appropriate thing to do in all situations, but if possible, it leaves the audience going out of your session having had a nice surprise. We all like nice surprises!

Even if you cannot plan for the "one last thing" moment, your presentation may still benefit from a "big moment" at some point. Is there a major announcement or big surprise? Is there something new that people are waiting for? The most successful presentations often have some moment within them where there was a big reveal; these are good at getting audience engagement.

In a typical scenario, you may find that there is an expectation that your presentation will end with a question and answer session. Providing an opportunity for the audience to ask questions and interact is important, but there may be occasions where this provides an ending that is more downbeat than you had hoped. I will deal with questions and audience interaction in more detail later in the book, but you may wish to consider how to end your presentation in this case. After all, the last part is what many people in the audience will remember the most. If you are having questions at the end, try to have a short summary or key message right after this. Particularly if there is a call to action, this may need to be the last thing that the audience hears before they leave the room.

The closing of the presentation needs to be short. If there is a feedback form or evaluation to be done, there is no harm in reminding the audience exactly how you have met the initial objectives during the session. While each attendee will make their own mind up about whether you were successful in meeting the objectives of the session, you can at least try to convince them that you have. Sometimes, this takes the form of repeating the objectives and then giving a few words about what happened in the session to meet them. My view on this technique is that you should judge the mood of the audience just before you do this. What can seem like a useful reminder can be very close to patronising your attendees. If the audience is on your side, then this technique can affirm that connection and the aims of the session. If they are not on your side, or the indifferent side of neutral, I would take great care in what I said in the wrap-up.

I should perhaps deal with how you plan to receive evaluations of your event from the audience. It is increasingly common for attendees to be emailed soon after the event, and fill out an online form. If you are planning to have your attendees fill in a paper evaluation form, then some thought should be given to how this will work on the day. If you provide the form during the closing part of the session, it is highly likely that people will start filling them in while the session is still in progress. They will end up paying little or no attention to what you are doing. You may well be constrained by protocols that you have no control over. In general, as soon as you mention the words "feedback" or "evaluation", people will find the form and start completing it. So avoid mentioning them until you finish. Better still, if the audience is not too large and logistics make it possible, you can have helpers distribute the forms at the very end, so that it is impossible to have them as a distraction. Whatever the set-up of the event, plan the end carefully so that there is no end-of-session housekeeping that conflicts with key messages and calls to action at the end.

Planning to deliver other people's content

You may encounter the situation where you are planning to deliver a presentation that someone else has written. You may consider that much of the planning has been done for you, and you would of course be quite correct. However, there are a few pitfalls with this situation.

You still need to make it your own, in order to deliver it in a convincing and engaging way. This means going through any notes that you have been supplied with and putting them into your own words. The process I described earlier of coming up with a comprehensive set of bullet points to work from still applies, so take the author's notes or script, and derive your own points. Clearly, you will need to remain faithful to the original. In this scenario, there is likely to be guidance on how much you can alter both the words used and the slides displayed. If possible, tweak them both to things that you are comfortable with. I can assure you that if you are not comfortable, then this will become evident to the audience, and could undermine the key messages.

If you are going to deliver a presentation that was not planned by you, you should establish carefully at the outset what the expectations are for you. In such a situation, there will undoubtedly be times when you will have to present content that is not how you would have done it, or slides that are not ideal. There are still plenty of techniques to maximise the effectiveness of the presentation, in terms of engaging with the audience. The key is not to let any deficiencies cause anxiety. You should also take extra care to remain professional during the delivery. It might seem funny or clever at the time to point out to the audience how poor a particular slide is, but if you are being compelled to deliver it, then the chances are that you are criticising one of your organisation's superiors, and that is never a good career move. It is also unprofessional to criticise your own organisation.

Using slides effectively

Once the content planning has taken place, you can start to put together the visual part of your presentation. For most, that will be slides from a software application such as PowerPoint® or Keynote®. I have seen some speakers mistakenly think that it is a measure of their presentational prowess that they can present and engage without slides. It is true that a good speaker can do this. However, they rarely seem to ask themselves if their presentation could have been better with a visual stimulus. I have already outlined the theory about preferred learning styles, and we should ensure that those attendees who prefer visual styles are catered for. However, we should also perhaps acknowledge that in presentations, content is usually delivered using a predominantly auditory style. If you think back to when you were young and being read stories, the story teller would often show pictures from the book to reinforce what was being said.

If you accept that presentations should contain some visual stimulus, then what should it be like? Before I answer that, I need to acknowledge another common situation that many presenters are faced with in a corporate environment. If you are representing your company, and it is not a small business, there is a fair chance that you will be subject to guidelines about your slides. You may be given a template to use, or worse still, a file that ought to be a template but is in fact just a sample slide. You may have certain extracts of text that you are expected to use. There may be presentational features that you are told that you cannot use. Most of the above is done out of a genuine desire to improve things. Medium and large organisations want some consistency and a uniform projection of their brand and corporate identity. That's fair enough. If you find yourself in this situation, you may end up having to select some of the techniques from this section, and not others. You may be able to break the rules for one or two slides only; the ones that you want to have a big impact and look different for that purpose. I also believe that organisations should be aware when their corporate identity on their slides is poor, and how you tactfully broach this with those co-workers who enforce mediocre templates is perhaps best left to your professional expertise.

There are a few general things to start with when designing a presentation. If the room is too light, slides with light backgrounds and dark text will be easier to see than dark backgrounds with light text. This is actually a good general principle, and has its basis in physics. Photographers will be familiar with the concept of depth of field and that more is in an acceptable focus when the camera aperture is small; it is similarly easier on the eye when the iris is small, hence my advice of using predominantly light-coloured slides.

A key principle of designing presentation slides is that their purpose is to reinforce what you are saying. As I mentioned earlier, people often remember what they see more readily than what they hear, so they can picture a memorable slide. Therefore, you should not try to make the slides do too much. I was tempted to say that you should not introduce new information solely on a slide without talking about it, and while this is often the case in effective presentations, this is not universally true. You may wish to have new information on a slide when using audience response technology or presenting numerical information.

I might run the risk of being accused of being pedantic with this next point, but I don't like visual content that is distorted unintentionally. You probably know what I mean, as it is the effect you see when a non-widescreen television programme is shown on a widescreen TV, and gets stretched horizontally. Circles appear as ovals, and all the people look a little overweight. The same is true of presentations. It seems that while widescreen televisions are the norm, it is still the old 4:3 ratio that dominates in presentations. Just to confuse matters, widescreen laptops often have screens that are in the 16:10 aspect ratio, compared to 16:9 for televisions. If you're thinking that this sounds like a bit of a rant on my part, you could be right. In short, when you create your presentation, ensure that you choose the right template with a display ratio that matches what you will be displaying it on. If in doubt, go for conventional 4:3. If you know it will be shown on a 16:9 monitor, choose a 16:9 ratio template. Then you will avoid your presentation (and particularly any pictures or videos) from being distorted. The correct aspect ratio is often ignored, but to me it is just another small thing that says to the audience "this is not as professional as it could be". That is not a comment that I would like made about me! I have seen professional audio-visual companies supply setups where the main projector was only capable of 4:3 and there were 16:9 monitors around the side of the venue. In such a case, you don't stand a chance. You would have thought they could at least have been consistent.

Perhaps I should finish the general comments by adding that rules can be broken, and some presenters use the breaking of common forms and conventions as a device to capture interest in itself. Nothing you read in this book should be considered as a commandment.

There are some "systems" that people operate for slides, such as having one slide for *x* minutes or *y* seconds of talking. I would argue that flexibility and variety are two of the key attributes of successful presenters. The pace of slides may vary depending upon whether you are supporting a recap of previous information or introducing something new. An information update may have a fairly brisk procession of slides, whereas the explanation of an idea may have a single slide displayed for some time. I will deal with timing later, but needless to say, flexibility is important.

Some key principles

If we believe that the purpose of the slides is to support what is being said, this needs to be achieved without the slides upstaging the presenter. I think there are a few key principles that characterise effective slide sets.

- If using bullet points, keep the number on each slide low, maybe three or four.
- Keep the text in each bullet point short and snappy. It should be a summary of what you are saying.
- Use the same font throughout the presentation.
- Keep all text large. If there is any text that cannot be read, remove it or change it.
- Avoid over-ornate lettering (or text as art), as it looks less professional (in my opinion).
- Avoid resizing images so that they end up being out of proportion.
- Avoid brightly-coloured backgrounds or backgrounds with brightly-coloured gradient fills.

Now many readers may be thinking "yes, I know all of that", and I suspect that nothing in the list is too far beyond common sense. But that does not then explain why I have sat through so many presentations by capable and professional people who know all of those points, but then do something different when they actually get to present. I think that part of the problem is that the purpose of the slides becomes diluted. They begin as a reinforcement of the presenter's speaking, but they are often printed and provided to attendees as notes. The temptation to then put too much on a slide can be great if they are viewed as a set of notes (which they are not). Effective speakers don't use their slides as surrogate notes. Presenters like Steve Jobs have only two or three words on their slides in some cases. If you want to give your audience notes, write them proper notes.

The power of pictures

The old adage, "a picture speaks a thousand words" has relevance here. In my opinion, many presenters do not make sufficient use of photographic images in their presentations, and most images are clip art in style. They are fine for simple things, but it is easy for the wrong clip art to make a presentation look like a school child's project rather than something aimed at business professionals. Increasingly there are many good quality picture libraries on the internet, and large organisations may well have their own stock photography service. Photographs look more professional and often appeal to the audience on a subconscious level. The challenge, as always with images, is to use them appropriately and in a way that enhances the overall effect. Don't just plonk a token photo on a slide and expect to wow everyone.

If you are following my advice and having two or three points on a slide, then there may be occasions on which the text can be substituted for photographic images. For example, in one of my presentations I was going to use a slide with three items that are relevant for effective presenters; a clear clock, a remote controller, and a microphone. Instead of having these as three bulleted text items, I decided to use a photograph of each one, but with the image of the item cut out from any background and placed on the slide. This can be a straight forward process in photo editing software for anything photographed on a plain background, and you may also find stock photographs of objects on a white background. The effect of this substitution was to make the slide easier to assimilate quickly, as everyone in the audience instantly recognised the objects. In addition, when referring back to the slide, it was easier for the audience to remember the slide content as it could be visualised in a way that text cannot be (as easily).

Another technique that has worked well for effective presenters is to use photographs as backgrounds to slides. This can be incredibly effective, as there appears to be a notable positive psychological effect of having people look at nice photographs as part of the presentation's visual stimulus. Also, using photographs as a background means that they do not have to be entirely related to the textual content of the slide. You can use them to make a point, or as a visual pun. As an example, I once used a photograph of the words "mind the gap" painted onto a station platform as a background for a slide on the gap in performance between different groups of people.

The other challenges when using photographs as backgrounds are ensuring that the quality is sufficiently good when viewed, having some space for the text, and ensuring that there is sufficient contrast between text and background. When using this technique, I tend to have a different photograph on each slide's background. This makes each slide something new for the audience.

When looking for suitable photographs, I firstly look for ones with some space where I think the text might go. The space needs not to have too many different colours in it; otherwise there will be trouble getting the text to be legible across all the area. I then tend to check what the resolution is. I'm looking for something larger than 1280 by 1024 pixels. If I have to resize it to be larger when inserted into the presentation software, then it is probably too small. I'm looking to resize smaller, not larger. Some of the general principles also apply here; avoid photographs that are mainly dark, as they will be lost if the projector is not sufficiently bright for the room.

Perhaps I should also add that if you are using photographs as backgrounds, the effect of adding further photos or clip art to the slide will be bad. Once you've got a photographic background, that's it for art work! You may also want to ask yourself if all the slides need a heading. While headings make navigating around the slides easier for the presenter, there are some slides where this is really superfluous information that should have been left out.

In my experience, adding photographic backgrounds has had a significantly positive impact on how presentations were received overall. If you've never tried this before, I would certainly recommend it.

Slide design

As you design your slides, the layout of objects on them will be a key consideration. For simple layouts, it is likely that your presentation software will handle most of the hard work for you. If the content is simple text or a graphic, you can probably choose a layout that is predefined in your software. However, there are likely to be slides where you are adding several elements yourself. How can you make these look attractive and easy to read? I have a few general principles that I use when laying out content on a slide. Having general principles is always better than trying to remember lots of individual examples.

- White space is your friend. Make sure that there is plenty on the slide. Of course, if your background is not white, the space won't be either! Text should have plenty of space around it. Try to have text spaced evenly, rather than crowded in one place.
- If you add elements manually, take a little time to ensure that they are aligned with each other. This is particularly true if you have several text boxes in a column, for example. Their left edges should all align. Get to know where the alignment tools are in your software.
- If you think you are about to put too much onto a slide, then you may already have done so.
- People tend to read from the top left to bottom right of a slide. Important items or the starting point of a diagram should be placed towards the top left.
- Symmetry can be used to make slides look more attractive. Use layouts that have some symmetry in content layout; for example, a single phrase will look better placed centrally on a slide than at the top. A small graphic may look better in the lower right corner, if balancing text that is mainly in the upper left. You can think of symmetry as providing some visual balance.
- Use "the power of three" to keep slides easy for the audience to digest. Whether it is three bullet points or three images, people tend to easily recognise patterns of three. You can extend this idea to having three areas for content. Keep the content tight in these areas, and it should be easy for people to assimilate.

If you have seen many presentations, then you can probably think of some examples of slides that were cluttered. Too many elements placed too randomly will make it more difficult for the audience to know where to look, and may take focus away from what you are saying at the time.

Charts and diagrams

If you have any numerical information in your presentation, the chances are that you are thinking about presenting it in a visual way. You'd be right to think that! But yet again, there seem to be some golden rules that everyone says that they know, but when actually in front of an audience, they get forgotten.

The first decision to be made is about the type of chart or diagram to use. Modern software will give you a bewildering array of chart types to choose from. You may have a chart supplied, although that does not necessarily make it the most appropriate type or suitable for your presentation. As a rough rule of thumb, I tend to use the chart types as follows:

Pie charts – good for data where the proportion of the total is the focus. If statistical accuracy is particularly important, note that 3D pie charts can give a misleading impression if the viewing position is too close to the side of the chart.

Bar charts and column charts – best for comparison of a set of figures. Choose a stacked chart if you wish to show how the proportion of contributions to the total has changed. For example, you might have a column chart showing how sales have changed over the past year. This could be done with a normal column chart. You could use a stacked column chart to show the same thing, but also the relative contributions of each department within the total. Clearly, the effect will be best with a small number of divisions within each column.

Line charts – show a trend in a numerical measure as it changes over time. However, if the interval between measurements changes at some point within the data being shown, the chart will be misleading.

X-Y scatter charts – this is the only chart type that will reliably show a relationship between two variables, and often used for physical relationships and hypotheses. They can be helpful in demonstrating a correlation between two factors. Note that line charts do not actually do this. For example, plotting the number of ice creams sold against the average daily temperature would provide evidence as to whether people buy more ice cream on hot days.

Radar charts – best for showing the relative amounts of aspects of one overall measure. For example, the relative scores of competency measurement for different areas in a performance management review.

Having decided on a chart type, you need to construct the chart in the software application. I have found that you often get better results by creating the chart in the presentation software and copying and pasting the data, rather than taking a chart wholesale from elsewhere. Charts copied and pasted from reports are often not suitable for presentations, as they are formatted for print and elements can be unclear or illegible from more than a few metres from the display screen. When formatting the chart, consider these points:

- Generally, have one chart per slide.
- Keep all text large. If it cannot be read easily, remove it.
- If text won't fit, consider rotating it so that it can stay large enough to be read.
- There is no need for a legend if there is only one set of data. If this is the case, remove the legend, as it is taking up screen space with no purpose.
- Ask yourself whether there is enough information on the slide to make the chart make sense. Each axis should be labelled

with what it is showing, and use numbers or text as appropriate.

- Any background should be considered more carefully than with a textual slide. The chart itself is already making the slide quite busy, so keep backgrounds simple.
- Make a suitable decision whether your axes should start at zero. This will depend upon the point you are making, but don't assume that the software has made the right decision.
- Don't try to present too much data in a single chart. Remember that the more attention that the audience has to give to working out what the chart is showing, the less they are giving to you as you speak.

Charts are one aspect of presentations that if you get them wrong, there will be people in the audience to whom you are instantly less credible. They are high stakes slides! Also, if there is a problem with a chart, people seem to be more likely to mumble about it rather than query it with you, so don't assume that an absence of questions equates with approval.

Builds and transitions

One of the difficult decisions about planning and creating any set of slides is whether to make use of build effects and transitions for the slides. There seems to be a wealth of conflicting common wisdom, so I will try to cut through it here.

The key point I shall make is that there is quite a variety of approaches that can work well. However, I have always found that the principle of not overdoing any one thing has served me well over the years. If you have taken on board my previous advice about having little content on each slide, you will be pleased to know that builds (where the content of the slide does not appear all at once) work most effectively when there is not too much on a slide. Some of the most effective builds I have seen and used in presentations are in fact for diagrams, rather than text. If a diagram represents a sequence or cycle, then having the diagram build up in stages can reinforce your commentary much more than showing the whole diagram at once. If the diagram is more than a very simple one, there is the risk that the audience do not know where to look first; a simple build can avoid this.

When it comes to choosing which of the many options to choose for a build, for either text or a diagram, you need to carefully consider the composition of the audience. In a business environment, whacky effects (such as letters dropping in one by one) provide an excessive distraction from the content. They may well have a place, but it is probably not when trying to leave a professional impression. In general, I avoid any build that reveals text one letter at a time. No matter how this is done, it always seems turgid as I (and I suspect most of the audience) are able to read faster than the slide can reveal the sentence. Fades and wipes are the most professional ones to use, in my opinion.

I've taken it for granted that it is fairly obvious what the purpose of a text build is; to show a series of points without the audience being able to see them all at the initial display of the slide. I tend to use builds only for certain slides, when I want a certain effects.

- When I want a bit of dramatic tension about what is coming next.
- When showing a later point would distract from an earlier one, typically when a later point adds more detail.
- When the points are part of a sequence, and I am explicitly or implicitly inviting the audience to think about what the next step might be, before showing them what I have on the slide.
- When there are key words that I would like to appear in time with my commentary.

This last technique can be quite effective. For example, if I were describing a new product or service, I might have two or three key words that describe it that I would like the audience to remember. If your timing is good and you are in full control of your slides, making these appear on the slide as you say them will make them much more memorable. However, again you need to consider your audience. I have seen this done in quite a crass manner, where the presenter dwelled on the fact that the words were to appear on the screen. Try not to do this in the style of a 1970's television advert either, where you announce each word. If you simply have them appear during your normal speaking style, then that is when they work.

Having confessed that I use builds for *some* slides, I must also confess that I use slide transition effects very sparingly indeed. I think that one of the worst crimes against the audience and presenter is the concept of a random transition. In other words, you have no idea whether the transition the computer chooses for you will be appropriate or excruciatingly embarrassing. Your look and gasp of surprise will never be taken as the action of a professional by the audience. Like elaborate textual art, random transitions should perhaps remain the preferred choice of the primary school child presenter.

I tend to use transition effects when I wish to punctuate my presentation, or demarcate one section from the next. Not all presentations will lend themselves to having clear and discrete sections, however. I also use a fade transition in some cases when there are slides with quite different backgrounds. It just eases the change on the eye. Where the slides have the same or similar backgrounds, I tend not to use them. I know that there will be some people reading this that use them all the time, and others who do not use them at all.

As I said earlier, my view on builds and transitions is that they can be used but not overdone. You should also think about the level of consistency between slides. Lots of different types of transition or build are distracting in a business environment. I used to use a "wipe from left" for builds in many of my slides. When I had used it once, I generally stuck to the same style of build for other slides where I wanted a reveal effect.

Animation

While animation tends not be used too much in business presentations, and rightly so, it can have a place. I do not believe that its place is for text, though. The only times I have seen or used successful animation is with diagrams.

A good diagram can be very useful. If you use Microsoft Office® productivity software, then the diagram creation got a lot better in the most recent versions than in older ones. If you have to present to an audience of any importance, particularly people from outside your organisation, this alone might be a good reason to upgrade. I would suggest keeping animations simple. There are some technical tips that I can provide that may help.

- Make sure that you know how to change the setting for when a build or animation starts. The default is likely to be for one following another, but you can set them to all start together.
- If the animation is getting hard to construct on a single slide, consider splitting it between two slides. Have the first part on one slide and the second on another, with no transition between the two.
- You can hide objects behind others by changing the stacking order. Explore the "send forwards" and "send backwards" options in your presentation software.

A well-judged and well-executed animation can wow an audience, but poor ones will have the opposite effect. If you develop an animation, show it to a colleague who you trust to give honest feedback, and if they have reservations, then remove it.

Video

Video is one aspect of presentations that seems to cause more problems than any other. A short video clip can have a welcome positive impact, and also gives you a short break from speaking. However, there are lots of things that can go wrong; the video may not display at all when the presentation is projected onto a screen, there may be colour issues, it may appear too small in the middle, or the aspect ratio may be incorrect.

As so much can happen when including video, I have put some of the technical details in an appendix. If you have video in a presentation, then it needs to work in as slick a manner as the rest of the presentation. That means not moving between applications during the presentation and having the video display at a suitably large size. It is possible in most presentation software to set a video clip to fill the screen when it plays, although few people seem aware of this. I think that the video needs to be as large as possible, and the audio needs to be of good volume at the back of the room when filled with people. I also tend to have a slide where the video will start as soon as the slide displays. This means that I do not suddenly have to find the mouse during the presentation. The most trouble-free launch of the video must surely be that when you click the button to advance to the next slide, the video will begin. I also tend to tell the audience how long the video is. This is part of managing expectations and removing the unnecessary elements of mystery for them. People seem to like that.

Once you have planned and developed your presentation, some thought should be given to the technology available on the day. My personal preference is to run a presentation from my own laptop, so that I already know exactly how it will appear. This may not be possible, or if you are speaking at an event with several speakers, the logistics may simply not allow for people using their own computers. In the case of copying your presentation to a CD/DVD or memory stick, there are a few potential pitfalls. I give my apologies to Keynote® users, as I will concentrate on PowerPoint® presentation software for a moment.

The most obvious pitfall is that media files for audio and video are not sorted as part of the presentation's file. When you add sound or video to a slide in a PowerPoint® presentation, it simply places a link to the file into the slide, and the link is a reference to where the file is on your computer. If you move the presentation to another computer, the media file will not be available. Luckily the solution is very simple; PowerPoint® presentation software has a pack and go option, where it will find all the files necessary for the presentation and package them up with the presentation itself. If you are using media files, this is a quick way to ensure that everything that you need for the presentation is copied.

There are some other more subtle issues. If you have decided not to use the default colour scheme in PowerPoint®, you may find that the colours of charts and diagrams are not what you expect when the presentation is run on a different computer. The text in a coloured box that was quite visible when you viewed it on your machine can suddenly be hard to read. The easiest way to check this is simply to run through the slides on the computer that will be used for the presentation itself.

If you are a user of Keynote® presentation software, then you may face similar issues. There is an option to save audio and movies within the file as part of the General options in the Preferences menu, which is selected by default. In the 08 version, your presentation was saved as a package, and you could right click it and choose to view the contents; this would verify that all the media was there. In the 09 version, you cannot inspect the contents using Finder unless you choose to save your presentation as a package (which is another option in the Preferences). Your media will still be saved in the file, so don't panic! To move the presentation, just copy the Keynote® file and all the resources should go with it. If you want to email the presentation and you are using a software version that saves everything as a package, then it may be helpful to right click the file and choose to compress it. This will create a copy as a zip file, which can be successfully emailed.

When choosing colours for elements on slides, bear in mind that the colours may not be as vivid when projected during your presentation as they were on your computer monitor. If the room that you are presenting in is not very dark and the projector is not very bright, combinations that may have had quite a good contrast ratio on screen can appear hard to discern. Always go for the best contrast you can, and always test the presentation on the actual equipment in the room you will be in, if possible, before the real session. This may not, of course, always be possible.

Humour

I would be avoiding a big issue if I did not make any mention of the use of humour as you plan your presentation. I could probably write a whole book about that (although for the time being, you will be relieved to know that I will not be doing so). I will start with the easy part. Unless you know your audience well, placing humour in the slides is probably best avoided. If for some reason the presentation is not going well, the last thing you want is a slide with a cartoon or joke on. I've seen this "finish off" struggling presenters. You should always assume that most people will not find funny the things that amuse you. My personal view is that cartoons on presentation slides (for a general audience) are rather naff, and no presentation I have seen in over twenty years has persuaded me otherwise. However, I should also say that a team leader using a cartoon with a team that he had known for several years went down well to lighten the mood, but then I suppose it is the exception such as this that proves the rule.

Things are a little different when it comes to what you say. If you set out to be funny (and you are not a stand-up comedian by trade), then you may have some hard times. Humour only works when the audience is on your side. When you see a stand-up comedian make it look easy, you must remember that the audience have paid to see that person, so they are already on his or her side, and already think that the comedian is funny. The audience that has paid to see something will be engaged from the start. It's a little different in a business presentation. It is unlikely that people will have bought tickets. Humour will not work if the audience is disengaged with you. If you stick to using humour in what you say, and not on the slides, then if the audience takes a little time to warm to you, you are not committed to using humour in the way you would be if it was in the content on a slide.

In my view, if you are going to use any humour in a business presentation context, it should be in the guise of a witty comment or amusing anecdote. Jokes *per se* are best avoided. If there is an anecdote that is short and reinforces the key messages, noting it down during the planning will help you if you feel it would be appropriate to use. Also, most effective humour feels spontaneous to the audience, even if it is not. If you do not think you can present it in a fairly spontaneous and relaxed manner, it might be best not to try. Even professional comedians who appear to be making it up as they go along usually plan and rehearse their work.

Finally, too much humour in a session that has serious messages can give the impression that you are not taking it seriously, or being overly flippant. There is a fine line between being amusing and trivialising the content and it is always safer to stay on the less amusing side of that line.

Before the day of the event, you should try a rehearsal of the slides. Go through all the slides, using your notes to give the points of the commentary. You will never quite capture the atmosphere of a real live audience, but you risk a lot if you don't go through everything at some point beforehand. With the advent of cheap webcams, you may even want to consider videoing yourself having a rehearsal. Personally, I cannot bear to watch myself on video, but it can be very informative as you notice all your own annoying habits and words that you repeat often without really being aware of doing so. If it is possible to rehearse in the room that the session will be held in with the actual equipment that you will be using, so much the better.

On the day

So you have your presentation notes ready, your slides composed, and the big day has come. It's downhill from now on? Well, no!

This is the part where I think the presentation should be treated like a performance. Therefore, the impression that the audience get at all times reflects on how professional they will perceive the session to be. Giving a professional presentation starts before the first attendee arrives. Obvious though it sounds, ensure that you arrive in good time, sufficient to test your slides on the actual setup to be used, and preferably early enough to be able to resolve any technical issues. Although you see it a lot, my view is that the audience should not have to watch people faffing about with equipment, setting up the slides, and so on. To me, that is rather like going to the theatre, taking my seat and then seeing the stagehands finish the scenery construction before the show begins. Even if there are technical problems that are completely out of your control, as the presenter you are the one who will look less than capable if things don't work, so best to get it sorted out of view of the audience. When the audience arrive in their seats, everything should be ready to go. Personally, my view is that if there are technical issues, I would rather keep the audience outside, enjoying their complimentary refreshments and having a chat, and then open the doors after the issues are resolved.

I'm going to assume for the rest of this chapter that you do not have any teleprompter or similar device. If you do, well lucky you! But back in the real world, how do we give our best when the session starts? I think that there are certain things that you need. You should be able to see what is showing on the main screen without having to turn to look at it, so a display facing you that is between you and the audience is essential. You also need to be aware of the time. There is an increasing trend for venues not to have a clock that is visible to the presenter. I can only assume that this is thanks to interior designers, who have never had to work in their own creations. For a professional presentation in a business environment, the presenter must be aware of the time and have clear sight of a clock. That clock should be easy to read. Other than that, it doesn't much matter where it is, although if it can be seen without having to obviously look at it, then so much the better. You should also have a glass of water to hand, as even the most experienced and engaging presenters sometimes get a dry throat half way through their session.

You may also need a microphone. I know that there are many who prefer not to use a microphone, but I think that unless you are in a fairly small room (with twenty or thirty people or fewer) you may need a microphone. Also, the shape of the room might make one necessary. I have presented to thirty people in a long, narrow room where those at the back had trouble hearing without a microphone. The "that's one more thing to go wrong" mentality is really just being a bit technophobic. Let's get some myths out of the way. It is not a sign of professionalism or competency if you can speak loudly to a room. You might be an asset in a noisy bar, but most professionals don't like being bellowed at. I have a fairly loud voice when required, but I always use a microphone if available. It is actually quite hard to sound relaxed when you have to raise your voice. It is also unwise to decide that you can be heard because one colleague can hear you at the back beforehand. When the audience are seated, it will be harder to hear you at the back, as some of the sound will be absorbed by the soft clothing of the audience members, not to mention that some people may not have as good hearing as your colleague. Finally, using a sound system is a courtesy to those who use hearing aids. Most venues of a reasonable size have hearing aid loops built in, and using the sound system allows attendees with hearing impairment to use those systems to get good quality sound from you.

If you use a microphone, a tie clip style one is often the best choice. However, take care with the placement of it if there is not a technician to advise you. It needs to be near the front of you; if it is too much to one side, the volume will vary too much as you move your head from side to side. Also, it should be away from any jewellery that might touch it. Finally, make sure you know how to turn it off, as the audience does not want to still hear you as you nip to the toilet.

Finally, you need easy sight of your notes, and be able to move on without too much trouble. It used to be the standard procedure to use index cards. As people found out, once you drop them, it is quite disruptive as you try to place them back in the right order in front of a restless audience. If you use paper, a print out of the notes pages of your presentation software application will probably suffice, especially if stapled or put in a slim ring binder. However, the default font size is often too small to be read from much of a distance, so increase the size of the note text before printing.

If you (or someone at the presentation) have a little technical knowledge, it may be worth exploring "presenter view" in your software. In short, this works by displaying different things on a laptop display compared to the external projector. Your presentation can display as usual behind you, but on the laptop screen you can see the current slide, your notes for that slide, and thumbnails of all the slides in the presentation, so that you can move to any slide quickly and easily. The notes also tell you what will appear next, which is useful not only as a reminder of the next slide, but if you choose to reveal points on a single slide. There are some advantages and disadvantages. If you will simply be showing slides, then presenter view can be useful. However, if you will be doing any demonstration that uses other software on your laptop, then you will quickly discover that it is more difficult in presenter view to do this. My advice would be to try it out if you have a chance to rehearse, to see how you get on with it.

At this point, I am going to take some time to discuss what might seem at first like a mundane issue, but in fact can make or break a presentation; that is, the simple advancing of the slides, and control of the presentation software. Sometimes, it is necessary to have someone else have control for you. This might be the case if you are unused to the software, or simply due to the logistics of the setup. However, if at all possible, I always like to have control of the presentation myself. In my view, it is better to learn how to use the presentation software and then have control than let someone else operate it. The problem with having another person advancing the slides is simply one of communication; how do you signal you are ready to move on? There are times when you may have a pacey sequence, such as an opening set, where the delay in asking for the slides to be advanced, or pressing a button that signals someone else to do it can have an impact, even if the delay is small.

As with all such things that I tend to have a little rant about, there are exceptions. If you will be demonstrating software, having another person actually operate the computer while you talk can often be the slickest method.

Given that in most circumstances, you as the presenter will be operating the slides, you need a method of doing so that is unobtrusive. I personally don't much mind people who stand behind a lectern and operate a laptop, or people who wish to move about. I tend to be a mover, as it were. An invaluable device for my presentations is a remote control for the computer. They are fairly cheap, and usually allow you to advance the slides, go backwards through the slide order and make the display black. Other than paying attention to the freshness (or otherwise) of the batteries in the remote control, there is little to go wrong. The main mistake tends to be pressing the button to advance the slides more times that you intend. Perhaps I just lack physical co-ordination. Such devices mean that the moving from slide to slide can simply happen when required, and is no big deal. You don't have to go back to the laptop, or ask someone to do it. The less attention you overtly draw to the change, the more professional your slide show will appear.

I have already made some mention of testing your slides in the venue before the start. There can be a few issues that may have an impact on how good your slides look. If using a different laptop to your own, you may find that fonts you have used are absent from the new machine and are substituted with something less suitable. You may find that there are subtle differences in the spacing of a substituted font that make the text flow differently. You may also find that the colour scheme you have used when authoring is not being used when presenting. Remedying these sorts of issues in front of an audience is never good, so do it beforehand.

Timing

I have mentioned earlier in this chapter the need to see a clock. This is because timing is an area where even experienced presenters can get caught out. Timing is hard to get right, but easy to get wrong. There are a few cardinal sins to avoid: Do not overrun into lunchtime. Do not overrun past the finish time. Either of these will annoy enough people in the audience to have an impact on the effectiveness of your presentation.

Keeping to the timing that the audience expects is yet again part of managing their expectations. Overrunning is by far the most common problem, and can be caused by factors within and outside your control. Overrunning is more likely when you have a complex presentation with many key messages, so my earlier comments about planning will help you stick to time. Sometimes a bit of an overrun is inevitable. Most people won't mind the odd few minutes, particularly if you warn them in advance when you realise your timing hasn't quite worked, and there are only five or ten minutes left. However, once you become ten, fifteen, or even twenty minutes over the expected end time, you have a problem. If you are part of an event with several speakers, giving the next person fifteen minutes less time due to your overrun is simply disrespectful. I am bewildered to this day why the serial over-runners don't realise that their actions are unprofessional and discourteous, particularly as they are often the people who complain the most about other things. Overrunning by more than a few minutes also sends some powerful negative messages to the audience about you and your work qualities. It can suggest that you are unable to be succinct when required, or that you are unaware of how long things take to present when planning.

So you should consider it a professional courtesy to both other presenters and the audience to keep as close to the planned timing as you can. In order to do this, I often have one or two parts of my presentations that I call the "DIY foam" slides. If you go to a DIY store, you will find that you can buy expanding filler foam that you spray into a gap. The foam then expands to fill the available space. I like to have at least one place in the presentation where there is some flexibility and the slide and associated speaking can fill the available space. If I am running behind, I can take a short time without adversely affecting the overall messages. But if I am ahead in my timing, I can usefully dwell on the points longer. This also highlights the folly of having timings that are too strict when you are working with an audience. Build in some flexibility in the planning stage, and place your "DIY foam" moments so that your presentation can expand to fill the available space.

Of course, there will be some occasions when your timing may not be as you want, due to a reason that is out of your control. A common example is when you are speaking after someone else, and they overrun. In such situations, I will often say to the audience "I have an hour's presentation for you, but as we are pushed for time, I will be cutting it down to around fifty minutes. However, it does mean that I might go over my allotted time by five minutes. I hope that's OK with you." Then I look to see if the audience members seem to be in agreement. I will quickly judge the mood in the room, and this often works as I am modifying the audience's expectations of what will happen. There are even occasions where you can enhance your own reputation by cutting an existing overrun down through being succinct and perhaps taking less time over some parts of your presentation.

One of the common causes of timing issues is questions from the audience. I will deal in more detail with this in the chapter on audience interaction. It is worth noting at this point that you should have a thought-out plan for dealing with queries from attendees. At all costs, you want to avoid them derailing the presentation. There is nothing that states that you must stop and answer all questions as they arise. Develop a strategy for dealing with questions, and let the audience know that their queries are welcome, but you will be dealing with them in a particular way. I sometimes like to present a section and then take questions at the end of that section; this is partly because some of the questions that attendees might have often get answered later in the section. Remember that you are in charge while you are standing in front of everyone. If you are being slowed by lots of questions, move on and arrange to deal with questions later. It's OK to do that!

Another key message that I would give regarding timing is "don't be too proud to have help". There are some occasions where, even as an experienced presenter, you know that there is an increased risk of the timing going wrong. In my experience, this can be when there are several activities, or when it is someone else's presentation and there is rather too much content that I am told to get through. In these situations, I will often ask a colleague at the back of the room to hold up their hand when there are five minutes to go. Whether or not I am able to finish in five minutes, it will refocus me.

So while we may have the planning and the mechanics of the presentation under control, the part that makes good presenters into great presenters is still to come; that is, how to engage with the audience.

Building a relationship with the audience

I don't want to build up this chapter too much, but the success of a presenter can be won or lost through audience engagement. For all the clever technology, great content and attractive slides, it is how you work with the people in the audience that will make for a great session and an effective presenter.

So let's get straight on to it. You have just got to the front; your first slide is ready. However nervous you may feel inside, an upbeat start is essential. If you haven't been introduced, make sure that people know who you are. Introduce yourself and what you do, related to the context of the presentation if possible. Try not to frown, perhaps even have a little smile.

As you speak, ensure that you speak clearly without mumbling, but not so loud that you are bellowing. Most modern venues do not have the echo-filled acoustics of old churches, so you do not need to speak particularly slowly. It is more about clarity than speed. Indeed, a slow speaking style can be quite soporific after a short while. It also makes you sound like a vicar giving a sermon, which is only fine if you *are* a vicar. I often think of the presentation situation as me simply talking to other people; there just happen to be a lot of them, and they probably won't talk back. So I speak as if I were speaking to a single person, in a conversational style, but just take care not to gabble or speak too quickly.

Most people use quite a lot of intonation when chatting with business colleagues. While best to not put it on too much, ensure that you speak with your normal intonation, so that your speech sounds natural. Sometimes I imagine that I am speaking only to one of the attendees. If you adopt this style, it gives you the opportunity to use verbal cues about the content of your presentation. When you get to a key message, or a really serious part, you can slow down and maybe even use slightly less intonation. As well as adding variety, this will signal to the audience the different status of that part of the session. Perhaps I can sum up the verbal style if I ask you to imagine that you are explaining something to a work colleague who you know and respect, but who is unfamiliar with the subject. As always, variety is good, so vary the pitch, volume and speed of your speech, although not too much. Try to reflect the variety that is heard when two people are having a conversation.

Be aware how you can change the volume of your voice. Again, important or significant messages can be slightly louder. You can speak more quietly for parts that you may want the audience to believe are more spontaneous comments, even if they are not. Keep your vocabulary straightforward and easy to understand. Every industry has its own vocabulary, which you can probably assume that everyone in the room will be aware of. But don't go too far, and avoid jargon and clichés. However, I am not suggesting that you "dumb down" what you say. Precision is still important, and will be valued by many in the audience, so if there is a particular term that may sound a little technical, you can still use it but you may have to expand upon it if you know that many in the audience are unaware of the meaning.

You will no doubt be aware of the huge volume of literature on the subject of non-verbal cues. These cues can be hugely influential on your audience, as they are often perceived to give away our inner feelings. Starting with the less sophisticated side of non-verbal behaviour, don't walk around too much, as it can be wearing to visually follow a person round for a couple of hours if they are constantly on the move. If you do find it more natural to move around, have periods when you stay fairly still, and times when you move in a small area. I also believe that the presenter should not move beyond the front line of the audience, unless doing some sort of audience participation. It is quite irritating as an audience member to have to twist your neck to see the presenter, when they could be standing in good sight of everyone. Think what you will do with your hands. I tend to "talk with my hands" and move them around a lot, and that is fine. Just have a conscious thought as to what to do with your hands if they are not holding something. I would not recommend putting them in your pocket though. As you are in control of the session, stand up straight and try not to slouch.

As you speak, don't concentrate too hard on looking at your notes. Remember that you are there to connect with people, so look at the audience for as much time as possible. Make eye contact with members of the audience as you speak, and particularly when you are making an important point. Try not to look at only part of the audience; make a conscious effort to make eye contact with people seated in all parts of the room. As you do this, you are making subconscious connections with members of the audience. If you notice that people in one area of the room are looking distracted or disengaged, try to make eye contact with one or two in that area. As well as the eye contact, you should be constantly visually scanning the audience to pick up on any signs that they are becoming restless. You can often determine from the body language of the audience members how well the session is going. If things are not going too well, or the audience is becoming disengaged, then you may notice that people are less likely to make eye contact with you. Their hands may be nearer their face, or they may be moving around a little more. Don't assume that if people are talking quietly to others near them that they are losing engagement. There are times when they may be commenting on what they have heard, and in fact their readiness to want to talk about what you are saying is a sign of engagement.

Whatever you do, you should try not to read to the audience. The idea underlying a presentation is that you have some expertise or message to bring, and the fact that you are presenting is going to somehow add value beyond the written materials. If you rely on reading your content, the audience will rightly conclude that anyone could have done that, and you are not really adding value. This is why I think that your notes should contain the points that you intend to make, rather than a script. Even more of a crime against the art of presenting is reading the content of a slide to the audience. If you are doing so because the writing was insufficiently legible, then that is your fault and you should have made the text larger. Reading from a slide is also a sign that there is too much text on the slide. Note though that reading from a slide is quite different to quoting a key phrase, which is something that you may do that will add emphasis to the key messages.

Depending on the context of the session, there will potentially be people in senior roles sitting with more junior colleagues, and it is natural that people will wish to ingratiate themselves with their bosses. However, more common amongst groups of similar ranking people will be the opinion formers. These are not necessarily the most senior people in terms of the role that they have in their organisation, but they are people whose opinions are most valued by others, and who influence others disproportionately. They may be people who have a particular expertise in their organisation, which may be related to the presentation content. In any presentational context that seeks to influence people, getting these opinion formers on your side can make for a much easier session, as well as ending up making for a more effective session. If you spot them, ensure that you make eye contact with these people.

Spotting these opinion formers can be harder than you think if you do not know the attendees. They are not necessarily the people who speak the most, ask the most questions, or talk the loudest. In my experience, they are often the people that when they speak, everyone listens to them. They don't monopolise conversations but often act to summarise discussion. These are certainly the people to talk to if you get an opportunity to meet the attendees informally. Don't assume that the person asking awkward questions is an opinion former; while they will ask if they have queries, they tend not to ask questions constantly.

As you are presenting, you should be constantly scanning the audience, looking for their non-verbal cues. This is why reading from a script or facing the main display screen for any length of time are not good things to do. If you are saying something that is going down well, you may find some people gently nodding their head in agreement, particularly when you make eye contact with them. They will tend to be looking at you or your slides. There are some tell-tale signs when an audience is starting to disengage from you. The reasons could be many and various; they may not like you, they may not like the content, or it may just be time for lunch. You will see things starting to happen, such as fidgeting, lots of "closed" body language (such as folded arms), whispering to colleagues during your speaking, people looking in many different places, excessive attention to hand-outs and notes. Picking up on these signs and moving on can save a presentation that is at risk of failing.

You may assume that the easy way to get an audience on your side and keep them there is to simply tell them what they want to hear, and agree with any points made. If you thought this, you would be wrong. I will spend some time discussing interacting with the audience in the next chapter. However, if you simply give in too easily or agree with a point that undermines something else that you have said (or are going to say), then you start to damage your credibility, and this ultimately damages your relationship with the audience. If there is an important point that is being challenged, often it can be best to stick to your guns, particularly if it is a small but vocal minority who are challenging you. If you do that, most people in the room will perceive that as a sign of strength or clarity of vision, if done with a bit of humility and without belligerence.

Enjoy yourself

A key part of being relaxed and in control is to enjoy giving the presentation. When you are enjoying what you are doing, there is a much greater chance of building a positive rapport with the audience. Of course, actually enjoying presenting is not as simple as saying it. We tend not to enjoy stressful situations. However, if you are enjoying what you are doing, this will be evident to the audience through a whole variety of verbal and non-verbal cues, such as body language, intonation of speech, facial expressions and language. It may sound like a cliché, but positivity from the presenter can indeed rub off onto the attendees. At the start of the session, you are setting the tone and atmosphere, and if that exudes positivity, then there is a greater chance that the session will be positive for the audience. This can work as positive feedback, where your demeanour influences a few people, who in turn influence a few near them. Please don't misunderstand me; being cheerful in the face of adversity is not what I am talking about. It is the subconscious messages that we all pick up when someone is genuinely enjoying what they are doing.

The other good reason for making every effort to enjoy your presenting is the positive feedback effect for you. When you enjoy presenting a session, your memories of presenting are then associated with a positive experience. We all have a strong desire to repeat pleasurable experiences, and the next time you have to present, you will already be expecting a good session. As your positive manner influences the audience, you have that good time that you were expecting, and the positive cycle is reinforced. Much the same is true with a negative cycle. Fear and stress make us present more poorly, so the session does not go as well, so we become even more stressed when the next one comes round.

At this point, you may be thinking that it is all very well for me to write about enjoying the experience of presenting a session, but it is rather harder in practise. The fact is that you may not enjoy it, and this is more likely if you have less experience at it. My response is to consider how the mind can work, and how powerful it can be. It is well known that states of mind can have physical manifestations. The *placebo effect* is one example, where people who are given a sugar pill instead of a medication still show signs of improvement beyond that from receiving no medication at all, simply because they believe completely that they have received medication. One example of the power of the placebo effect is in pain relief. An American anaesthetist, Henry Beecher, wrote about his experiences working in a field hospital in the Second World War. At one point, all the morphine had been used, so saline solution was used instead, but the patient did not know that it was not morphine. The patient was fine, to the amazement of Mr Beecher. This is not a trivial effect, as I would imagine that the pain from war wounds is significant. There are other examples of the power of the placebo effect in medical procedures, as well as examples of people feeling unwell because they expected to, rather than because they were exposed to something that would make them unwell. However, I use this simply to serve as an example of how powerful the mind can be in our well-being.

The process of enjoying a presentation that I know could be stressful starts early. When I think about it, either because I am preparing or because I am made aware of the session, I visualise it going well. I picture myself with the audience having a successful session. I always ensure that there is sufficient planning time, so that any possible issue that could cause anxiety can be dealt with beforehand. I also try very hard to take a particular view of possible mishap, in that if something goes wrong during the session that I have not foreseen, then there may be little that I can do about it, so I should not get stressed about it. As you think about the session, think about parts of it that will go well. Focusing on what *might* happen is often not useful, and can create anxiety. However, thinking about elements that you have prepared carefully, knowing that they cannot be derailed will build confidence.

It is natural and right to be nervous prior to a presentation. Experienced actors report that they often have terrible nerves just before a performance. However, knowing that being nervous is natural can help. There is a difference between being nervous about how the session will go, and being unnecessarily anxious about it. In those minutes prior to speaking, keep determining that you *are* going to enjoy it, despite whatever anyone says or whatever happens. The more you can really believe it, the more likely it is to actually happen. Try to look forward to the session, and think of all the positive benefits of doing it.

Try to avoid objects or routines associated with negative experiences. Our minds work in a fundamentally associative way, which is why people get on so well on the web with the idea of hyperlinks. We all know how a sound or a smell can evoke strong memories of past events. Sometimes, there is a particular thing that we do when we are stressed or uncomfortable; it might be having a particular drink or food stuff. The problem is that these things end up being associated with negative outcomes, and provide the framework for our mind to determine that a negative experience is likely to happen. By way of example, when I was at university, a friend of mine was training to be a teacher. She was doing teaching practice and had a particularly difficult class. In order to settle her nerves, she would have a cup of herbal tea beforehand. The problem was that the tea became synonymous with an unpleasant experience, to the point where she told me that just the smell of herbal tea would make her feel slightly sick. The act of drinking herbal tea caused stress and anxiety as she had become conditioned that the tea was a prelude to an unpleasant experience. If you have your equivalent of the herbal tea from the example, try to remove it from your routine before a presentation. Your conscious mind may be telling you that it will calm you down and soothe you, in reality your subconscious mind may be shouting "hold on, we're in for a bumpy ride".

As you speak, you give away small subconscious messages about your views and interest in what you are speaking about. It can be your body language that does this, but even the vocabulary that you use can play a part. To be fully effective in your speaking, you need to have a genuine interest and passion for the subject that you are talking about. We behave differently when we are enthusiastic about something. Of course, you can overdo this. If your audience is indifferent, an excessive display of passion can switch them off and seem cheesy. The most engaging presenters are those that believe in what they are saying, so ensure that you are committed to the key messages in your presentation. After all, you are the person who, in the eyes of the audience, has been chosen to deliver them. Deal with your own doubts before the session, and ensure that any queries you have yourself are resolved.

In summary, try as hard as possible to *believe* beforehand that the session will be a positive and enjoyable experience. Know that you do not need to act, or try to be someone else or something different to yourself. You are simply bringing out the inner presenter in you. Being yourself with the audience is the best way to enjoy what you are doing, as a façade will never fall in this case. Try to believe that it will go well and that it can be enjoyed. Remember that the presentation is likely to be an opportunity for the audience to gain the benefit of your expertise and experience, and that should be pleasurable for both you and them. In short, you can think your way to enjoying what you are doing in the presentation.

Handling audience interaction

Often the aspect of business presentations that presenters fear most is dealing with members of the audience. It's not really like stand-up comedy, where a witty put-down is all it takes. The audience is made up of your fellow professionals, and in anything other than a large event, will expect some way of interacting.

Handling questions

Dealing with attendee questions can seem quite innocuous, and yet I have seen this aspect of presenting completely derail a session. The way in which you deal with questions and queries not only affects your own reputation, credibility and status in the session, but can either build or destroy audience engagement.

Perhaps the most obvious point to make first is that every member of the audience should be treated with respect. This is irrespective of how daft their question is, how good or bad they are at their job. Showing disrespect to an attendee will always raise a few eyebrows, as others will be thinking "that could have been me". Of course, respect does not equate to agreeing with everything someone says.

Before your session, part of the planning should be to give some thought to how you will handle questions. If you have a small group of people, then you may wish to take questions as they arise. The problem with this approach is that often people will have a query that is addressed in a later part of the presentation. You can of course simply tell them this, although if I tell someone that the answer will be coming in a few minutes, I also tell them that they are welcome to ask again if the planned elements of the presentation have not fully answered their query. For most presentations with more than a handful of people, you may find it desirable to tell your audience that there will be opportunities for questions after each section of the presentation. By making people wait, it forces people to think a little more about their question as they have to remember it or write it down. This can help avoid some "spur of the moment" questions from attendees that add little to the session. There will be times when an attendee simply "gets the wrong end of the stick", and if they have to wait a few moments before asking about it, they may realise what their misconception is and hence avoid humiliating themselves in front of everyone. If the session is fairly short, or part of several presentations in an event, it may be best to set aside the last five or ten minutes for questions from the audience, and ask them to save their questions for then. One technique that I saw used well was where attendees were invited to write questions on sticky notes, and place them on a flipchart whenever there was a suitable moment. The presenter would then group them and respond to them at the end. This reassured those contributing questions that their query would be dealt with in the session.

When you get a question or query, they will tend to fall into one of several categories. The easiest to deal with will be the simple "clarification of a point" type. Despite being easy to deal with, I have still seen presenters do a bad job with this type of query. If an attendee has not fully understood something in the presentation, simply repeating it is less likely to be helpful than thinking of a different way of explaining it. When you get this type of query, try to explain the point in question using different vocabulary, or from a different starting point. If you present the same content several times and get similar queries, that is a sign that the subject of the query has not been dealt with well in the presentation, and you should consider making some revisions if you are presenting the same session in the future.

Another type of question that you are likely to face is the "related question". Again, these can be fairly straightforward to deal with, and usually occur when something you have presented prompts a thought in an attendee's mind about a slightly different scenario. These sorts of questions on relevant, related situations are easiest to answer if you have a good knowledge and understanding of the field that you are speaking about. This is why a good presenter is not just a type of actor. A good response to this type of question can really boost your credibility with the audience. If you are unsure of how to answer a question on related material, resist the temptation to guess. In my experience, people have more respect for someone who will go and find out an answer over someone who guesses and ends up being inaccurate or wrong. I have had a situation where I had a tricky question and I really did not have a definitive answer, so I offered to phone a colleague who would know during a break. I did so, and reported the answer back to the audience. This type of response showed that I was willing to put a bit of effort into ensuring the audience have the right information.

A popular type of question with some attendees is something that sounds like a question, but is actually a point of disagreement. It is often only professional protocol that prevents the questioner from simply stating their disagreement. These people can be tricky to deal with, depending on the nature of the disagreement. Firstly, don't assume that the questioner is representative of the whole audience. A common mistake of inexperienced presenters is to assume that those who speak up are representative generally of the opinions and mood in the room. This is not necessarily the case. Also, disagreements with the presentation content can sometimes arise from a perception by the attendee of implied criticism. My response tends to vary depending on the extent to which the disagreement is based on facts, or is an opinion. The view that I often take with a difference of opinion is that the attendee's opinion is valued, but simply different to my own. I may restate some facts that I think back up my own opinion. The really important point about disagreement style questions is not to get drawn into an argument. If you think that this is about to happen, then offer to speak to the person concerned after the session. Resist the temptation to be too hard on disagreeing attendees. It may just be that they think that you have not considered a particular fact or point, and you may just have to reassure them that you have.

An overriding principle is to try not to let one or two people hog the discussion. You may have to be firm or offer to speak to people afterwards, in order to allow as many as possible to ask a question. If a questioner makes a good point, or asks a good question, you may comment on that, partly as a sign of respect, that the question is not a silly one. If someone does ask a silly question, or it is clear that they have not grasped a key principle that everyone else has, I sometimes apologise that I had not made the point sufficiently clear, and then attempt a different explanation. As a presenter, you are not trying to portray a veneer of invincibility, and implying that their lack of understanding may be down to you removes any implication that they have asked a silly question. Of course, you may have to accept that your explanation was indeed not up to scratch if the questioner is greeted with nods and grunts of approval when they ask.

You will also occasionally get the off-topic question. For me, the key consideration is the extent to which a response will derail the overall presentation, waste time, or distract the audience's attention away from the key messages. In other words, if you are not pushed for time and you can give a fairly swift response, you may want to offer an answer. If, however, it is likely to prompt other off-topic questions or you are tight on time, you will need to politely deflect the question; offer to speak to the person afterwards, or email a response to them. Ensure that it is clear to the audience through your language and manner that you are not brushing off the question, but it is perhaps a query that does not need to have time spent on it with the whole audience in attendance.

Activities

With smaller groups, activities are an often-used device to build and maintain interest and engagement. I am afraid that I could probably write an entire book on the subject of activities in presentations and events, so I shall try hard to be concise. What I shall not do (in any detail) is discuss the various different types of activities that can be done in conferences, seminars, etc.

The first, and biggest, question that you should ask yourself is whether activities are appropriate and how much activity should be included. This is not quite as straightforward a question as it seems, as there are several factors that should influence this decision:

- What type of session is it? While activities are a desirable element of professional development sessions, they are less appropriate for a product launch.
- How is the room arranged? If you have your audience sitting at tables, activities are going to be more appropriate than if they are in rows.
- How many people are in the audience? If you want feedback from an activity, this could be slow and tedious for a large number of people.
- What are the expectations of the audience? If they are not expecting an activity, it is not always a pleasant surprise to find one included. If they are expecting a session where they will receive information, an activity may not always go down well.
- How long is the session? The attendees should not feel that an activity is wasting their time. If you include an activity and are then pushed for time for other parts of the session, the attendees will question why you spent the time on the activity. If you can justify it, however, that is fine.

Not least among the factors you consider should be the practicality of an activity. One of the most basic errors I have seen several times is when there is simply not enough space for people to perform an activity easily.

If you have considered the factors above and decided to include an activity, then I think there is one critical requirement; it must have a clear purpose, and it should be clearly linked to the aims and objectives of the session. Not only that, but the purpose and relevance need to be explicit to the audience. No one likes to feel that they are simply being kept busy for the sake of it. Don't be afraid to conclude that activity would not be appropriate.

The other requirement for an activity to succeed is for it to avoid *faff*. That is, it needs to be able to run in an efficient manner, without too much fuss. If the whole activity, including any feedback from it, cannot be run efficiently and with a brisk pace, then it will probably have a negative effect on the overall session. This means that if any stationery is required, then ensure that attendees have it before they need to start. Note that I have mentioned *efficiency* rather than *duration*. The timing of activities is notoriously difficult to get right, and it is almost a no-win situation. Some attendees will inevitably decide that it was too long or too short for them. Efficiency does not necessarily mean quick and short, although longer activities tend to characterise professional development sessions more than other types of presentation.

If you plan to gather feedback, I think you need to consider whether you need to, and what you want from attendees that will move the session forward. I have seen many activities go very well until the feedback phase was started. At that point, the pace slows, and sometimes you can find that one or two of the louder voices can monopolise the feedback. Again, can this be done efficiently? I think that feedback should have a clear purpose, just as the whole activity did. Sometimes, the purpose of an activity may simply be to give people space and time to reflect on something they have just heard, and if that is the case, then feedback may even be non-existent.

Gathering feedback on a flipchart can be problematic if the audience is large, and ideally the writing should be done by someone else, so you as the presenter can maintain the focus and pace rather than worrying about writing on the chart. One of the issues with flipcharts is that if you want attendees to take away the main points of feedback, there is a delay and you have to get the chart typed up and sent out. One strategy that I have found works well is to use a digital camera or camera phone to take an image of the chart, and then post the chart into a shared online area. Since this can be done quickly, attendees can get the information while they are still thinking about the session, and it avoids transcription errors.

Once an activity is running, the main challenge is likely to be to keep everyone in the audience on-task. Depending on the context, you may decide to accept some off-task behaviour provided that it is still useful activity, but most of the time you will want attendees to be working on the task as given to them. It is fairly obvious that disinterested and disengaged people are much more likely to go off task. If your session is going badly, there is at least a fifty per cent chance that an activity could kill it completely. If you have noticed that the audience have not engaged, think very carefully before providing the opportunity for them to disengage entirely and check their email. Keep them on-task by moving around amongst them, if possible. Beware of being "captured" by responding to a query in one part of the room and then not being able to get away for some time. As you move around the room, be listening to what people are saying as you pass them, and try to determine if there are many people going off-task. Don't be afraid to finish an activity early if you detect that people are not engaging with it. However, you may just need to re-state what the task is if the reason for disengagement is confusion over what to do.

Finally, activities can work well when they inform what happens later in the session. Attendees can feel engaged when something they have said or done affects an element of what comes next. If there are places in the session where you can refer to the outcome of an activity or some feedback from the audience, make sure that you do so. Make it fairly explicit, for example, "I'm going to spend a little longer on this part since people mentioned that they wanted to know more about it" or "I'll deal with this quickly as I can tell from the activity that you are already familiar with this". However, business presentations are not like school classrooms, and you should assume that the audience have a higher tolerance for working in plenary.

Audience response systems

With the advent of more cost effective consumer electronics, we have had the rise of the audience response system, or voting system to give it its colloquial title. In a typical scenario, the audience are provided with small handsets with which to provide quick feedback, or to engage in a quiz. There are different systems available of varying complexity, but they all have in common the ability to pose a question and get fast responses from audience members.

One fundamental mistake that some presenters make when using such devices is to assume that their very presence in the session will engage. This is true to some extent, but the novelty will quickly wear off if they are simply a gimmick or time filler. As with other activities, the use of an audience response system should have a clear purpose within the context of the session.

There are two technologies that are used by the handsets to send the attendee responses; infra-red and radio. The systems that use radio signals can be susceptible to interference, but tend to be more robust in my experience. They do not require the attendees to orientate the handsets in any way to point at a receiver, and typically have a longer range than infra-red devices. However, they may be more expensive to rent or buy, although the price difference is getting less. If possible, my preference tends to be for the radio systems. However, if you are on a tight budget, then the infra-red systems could suffice. They work on a similar basis to a television remote controller, so they usually need to be pointed towards a receiver. For a smaller group, or smaller room, they can work just as well as a radio system. The best systems have software that will integrate with your presentation software application, so that there is no switching around of equipment or software applications needed during the presentation.

As a device for improving engagement, they can be very effective when used in the right way. They give the powerful combination of an activity but with quick feedback (which can easily be saved or manipulated). Like any activity, some care should be taken when thinking about using an audience response system. The questions asked should be directly relevant. Think what conclusions you want to get out of the responses as you start designing the questions. Most audience response software can get quite sophisticated, but keep things as simple and straightforward as possible. The only element of sophistication that I have found to be useful is separating answers by demographic, although this is something that is best done in analysis afterwards. You can ask people about some aspect of their role. For example, in an audience of education leaders, you may ask people to respond in the first question to whether they are a head teacher or from an education authority. Then you can see if the two groups responded significantly differently to the questions.

When it comes to the questions, the advice I have given about slides in general also applies. Keep the questions short and clear, and don't provide too many possible answers. Clearly, the multiple choice format of these systems will limit what can be asked. I am not so keen on the ability to present a ranking exercise, as unless the handsets have a display, audience members are not always sure that their button press has been registered, which can result in erroneous results. When I have used these systems, I usually start with a fairly unimportant question that I use to familiarise the audience with the system. I will explain how the system works, which is usually pretty simple. Most of the time, you as a presenter will open the voting by showing a slide or pressing a button on the computer's keyboard. The audience can then vote for either a specified time or until you close the voting. I tell the audience that the first question is a rehearsal for them. It also can serve as a reassurance to audience members that they have voted successfully.

The key to maximising on the engagement that these systems will bring you is to maintain the pace and purpose of the voting session. It may provide an opportunity for a little entertainment, particularly when you reveal the results. There is absolutely no reason why you can't have a bit of fun, as long as it does not detract from the key messages and is appropriate. For example, I would not have much in the way of fun when presenting about redundancy options, but I might if presenting about a new service. Keep the session going, and don't necessarily wait for everyone to respond; there may be some who don't wish to respond or cannot do so, and keeping everyone else waiting for too long will slow the session down too much. I used to find that there were always one or two people who would not register a response in a timely way. As long as the vast majority have voted, don't wait for ages for the very last vote. The exception to this would be a situation that is politically sensitive in your organisation, where there might be a reasonable expectation that everyone's response is being taken into account.

There is an inevitable question that arises whenever I talk to people about technology; what if it doesn't work? The answer is very simple, and that is to move on quickly. I have seen even experienced presenters get into quite a stressed state when some piece of technology fails to work. Everything stops, the pace is lost, and while the presenter and their helpers attempt to sort out the problem, the audience are left to talk among themselves and generally lose focus. In the case of an audience response system that decides to mutiny during your session, my advice would be to simply leave it. If there is an opportunity for someone to help and to sort out the problem while you and the audience are doing something else, then that is very useful. But if it isn't going to work, then leave it and move on. Ask yourself whether it really matters. It may be true that something about the session will be lost, but the key messages and big ideas should be bigger than any one piece of the presentation. Those things ultimately come from you, and hopefully there is nothing that will stop you from presenting them during your session. I have sometimes had the odd technical glitch. If there is an opportunity to remedy the problem, for example during a refreshment break, you might say to the audience that you will be trying to get it working and will come back to it later (if it is desirable to come back to it). This type of approach makes you appear in control. Rather than let a malfunction worry you, you are working around it and determining what will happen.

One of key characteristics of audience response systems that I consider to be useful is that the results can be saved and analysed at a later date. While quizzes may be fun, these systems make gathering feedback relatively painless for the audience. In a business environment, your co-workers can be given a voice with an audience response system, and whether they like what they hear or not, people usually react more rationally when they feel that they are listened to.

Slides, but not as we know them

There are many situations when the linear set of slides is the most appropriate way of providing a visual backup to your session. However, there are new ways of presenting slides to an audience, and the possibilities increase as time passes. There are many new approaches to presentations coming to the public arena, but I will concentrate on just a few.

The first I shall consider is an add-in for the PowerPoint® presentation application. Again, I apologise to users of the Keynote® presentation application for concentrating on a different product, but I hope that you will forgive me as this is a development that should be of general interest. The add-in is called pptPlex and can be downloaded from Microsoft's web site. When used, the effect is rather like having a large table with the slides spread out across it. The slides can be grouped into sections, which correspond with the sections of the presentation. You can zoom in to a section, and also to individual slides. As you move from slide to slide, the display pans across. As a presenter, you can show your slides in order, but you also have the option of zooming in and out at will.

As a presenter, this gives you the opportunity to run your session in a non-linear way. If there is some feedback from the audience that they are particularly interested in a certain aspect of your subject matter, you could zoom into a set of slides that gave additional detail. It also performs a task that I have mentioned earlier, and that is telling the audience where the session is headed and what they are going to expect. Everyone will see at a glance what the various sections are, and roughly how many slides are in each one.

Creating a presentation using this add-in is very straightforward. Once you have downloaded and installed it, you will see a new ribbon available to you in the PowerPoint® application. When using this add-in, I tend to start by having all the individual slides completed, and then adjust it for pptPlex. The first thing you will need to do is to create sections for your presentation. This is achieved by adding sections using the Home ribbon. Each section can be renamed by right-clicking the section heading and making the appropriate selection. Each section you create will correspond to a group of slides in your pptPlex.

Once you have your sections set up, you can turn your attention to the pptPlex ribbon. The virtual table on which your slides will be placed is called a canvas. As you add a canvas, you can select a background or use a background of your own. The canvas will be added as the first slide of the presentation. It can be altered by moving and resizing the placeholders for the sections. Once you know how many sections you have, I tend to delete the unneeded placeholders, and move and resize the remaining ones to cover the canvas evenly. When you start your pptPlex from the overview, you will see the whole canvas. The first time you start the overview, it may take a little while for all of your slides to be processed. On subsequent occasions, the start will be a lot quicker.

Full directions for moving and zooming can be found in the pptPlex web pages. I suggest that you practise beforehand. You will also need to be at the computer that the presentation is running from, or have easy access to it (or have a very well-trained assistant).

It is worth having a look at the advanced options that are available. You can change how the slides are arranged in each grouping, and how the display moves between them. As with many such software applications, it will look best to the audience if the computer running the slide display is fast and powerful enough to be able to zoom and pan smoothly.

Another new way of presenting takes the idea of pptPlex one stage further. It is known as Prezi, and can be found online at prezi.com. As with all online web applications, I should start with a disclaimer, that this application and web site are owned and run by a third party. Therefore, information about it may change, and features that I refer to may be altered, added to, or removed.

As with pptPlex, you can pan around a canvas, and zoom in and out to content. You can group content and even import a set of PowerPoint® slides. However, you are able to position individual elements directly onto the canvas, such as text, images and shapes. This means that your visual content has a much less "slide like" appearance. My personal view is that the interface for designing presentations is very easy to use. Resizing and rotating elements is very easy and intuitive. The other significant feature is that all of this happens in "the cloud", in other words, your work is stored on servers on the internet, and you work with and display your presentation using your web browser. You can define a path through your content, or manually navigate around in a non-linear way, again allowing for a more spontaneous and reactive experience for your audience.

Without wanting to spend too long getting into the advantages and disadvantages of using cloud-based applications, it is probably worth considering what this might mean in a typical business presentation scenario. My experience is that most conference venues have wireless networking capability, as do most offices. One advantage of having your presentations stored remotely is that you can access them from any machine with internet access, and it will look and behave the same as it did on your computer. The obvious disadvantage is that if you don't have internet access, you cannot use your presentation. Luckily, Prezi provides a way round this, and has a desktop application. You can download your Prezi and then use the application to show it when you are offline. I think that if I were going to use it in a high stakes environment, I would do this. At the time of writing, the desktop application is a paid-for option after an initial free trial period.

I should also point out that the free accounts do not have an option to make the presentation private; it is clear when browsing the site that some users have not realised that their work is public. If you are working with a free account, you will need to be careful about including information that may be confidential, privileged, or commercially sensitive.

Like pptPlex, you will need access to the computer running the presentation, or a very well-trained assistant, in order to manipulate the presentation. Clearly, it is worth rehearsing the presentation and becoming confident in controlling it if you anticipate adding a little spontaneity to your session.

The "back channel"

I am finding it increasingly common for presenters to use social media to promote and follow up their work. I have also seen social media such as Twitter used so that attendees could comment on the presentation as it was in progress. This is a relatively new use of such media and I have mixed views on how it affects the engagement of the audience.

Clearly, providing an extra communication channel for audience involvement is a good thing. Attendees can raise questions, make comments, and interact using a wide range of devices. Increasingly, all an attendee needs in order to interact during a session is a smartphone. Before the presentation, using social media to pose questions and make points that you could address in your session is a useful addition to the set of tools available. I do, however, have some reservations about certain practices that are becoming more common.

I have attended a large conference where there was a Twitter feed displayed on the large screen behind the presenter during the session. Attendees Tweets were displayed, and updated in real time. All attendees had to do was ensure that their Tweet included an agreed *hash tag*. For the uninitiated, hash tags are keywords prefaced with a hash symbol (#) that allow you to find associated Tweets. The hash tags do not need to be set up in advance, which makes Twitter a responsive and fluid network (which is a good thing). As long as attendees include the agreed hash tag in their Tweet, you should be able to find it. It was an impressive display of technology enabling audience interaction, but I was left wondering what it had done to the impact of the presentation and the engagement of the audience. It is easy to guess where the audience attention was for most of the time; that's right, reading the Tweets and not paying as much attention to the presenter. There was also the issue that anyone could post anything. Some people were posting Tweets who were not actually in the session, but their comments still appeared. As a member of the audience, I felt that the presenter was being undermined, not by the comments themselves but by the drawing of attention away from the speaker.

Despite the unease that I felt, I knew that using Twitter in this way was going to have great potential. My advice on using such services is based around maximising engagement, rather than concentrating on the service itself. First off, I should say that I only consider it to be appropriate where you have a large audience. In other words, if the audience is small enough that you can take questions and feedback directly and personally without adversely affecting the flow of the session, then do so. In a large conference situation, the use of Twitter needs to have a little management in order to secure its effectiveness. Before (or at the start of) the session, agree a hash tag for everyone to use, and to filter the Tweets on. As you start, the Tweets will begin to come in.

If you do not have someone who can assist you, then you will need a second device (other than the computer displaying the presentation) to view the Tweets, with appropriate software. There are many applications that will show an animating display of Tweets updating in almost real time; you merely need to do a search of the web to find them. While you are presenting, you can glance at the Tweets and respond as appropriate. I suggest that you make reference to the Tweets or respond to some fairly early on so that the audience know that you are getting them, even if they can't see them themselves. Of course, a better arrangement is to have an assistant monitoring the Tweets and picking out common themes and questions, and communicating these to you at appropriate points in the session.

Don't worry about collating the Tweets or distributing them, as anyone can see the Tweets online at a later time. You might want to remind your audience that unless they have changed the settings on their Twitter account, their Tweets are public and therefore can be viewed by everyone on the web. Not only that, but it is clear who submitted the Tweet. This may be necessary as I still come across people who appear to think that their Tweets are private by default.

I would also caution against using social media generally for feedback. It is certainly nice if people Tweet that they enjoyed the session, or it was useful. However, my view is that this type of feedback does not replace adequately the sort of carefully planned feedback that you would want. I would also question whether people will feel that they can be candid with you when their feedback is potentially in the public domain. While many may feel uncomfortable giving public feedback, you can also be sure that those with something negative to say will be more than happy to air their views in a public manner. In my experience, some of the most useful feedback on presentations has been given by attendees in the section where free comments are allowed (as opposed to the usual ratings of various attributes of the session). It is precisely these types of comments that are less likely, in my experience, to be put on public view.

The main point about social media is that they should complement the presentation and not distract from it.

Presenting online

With the rise of web software as a service, and the trend towards more employees working at home, there has been an increase in the amount of online presenting. Clearly, there are many parallels with presenting to a group when both parties are physically in the same room, but equally there are some nuances to online presenting. As with presenting in person, it is not always the case that the audience will be engaged. One feature of online presentations is that the audience tends to be relatively small, if only for cost or technological reasons.

There are two methods of presenting online. You can use simple screen sharing software, and have a telephone conference call for the audio. This can work well when there are only a few people to present to, but for most presentations it is desirable to have a little more control over the proceedings and a greater feature set. Most presentations will use software that is designed for online meetings, that provides a virtual meeting room to conduct the presentation in.

There are slightly different common conventions for online meetings. For a start, most online systems require a person to act as host for the session. This person is typically the one who has set up and scheduled the meeting, and they have the greatest level of control over what happens. Many systems also require the host to be present in a meeting. If you are working in your own organisation, then you may well be the host, but if you are speaking in an online event where you are one of many presenters, you probably are not. In addition to the host, in most online meeting systems, the participants can be given different roles, or sets of permissions. If you are presenting a session, you will usually be given an enhanced set of permissions; the role is usually called *presenter* or *moderator*. This will usually give you control of more of what everyone sees, and often enables you to be heard when others are muted.

At risk of stating the blindingly obvious, you should practise using the software before the event. If rehearsing was important for a standard presentation, then it is even more important for an online event. You need to verify that your computer can run the software and that your internet connection is good enough. Some systems may require you to download some software to your computer in order to share certain types of content, or to share your desktop. You should also check that the hardware that you intend to use works and that it co-operates with the online meeting software. Although it seems obvious, I have been in several online meetings where participants have been unable to get their microphone working so that they could be heard. Nowadays, blaming the computer or the software is not really going to help; that type of problem reflects on the person, and your credibility will suffer if that happens to you. If you are not sure how to test your speakers and microphone (or headset) prior to the meeting, don't be afraid to ask someone who may know about the system being used whether you can have a test session at some point beforehand. My personal preference is a headset, especially as they can be bought fairly cheaply these days. As well as ensuring that you can hear well, and the quality of your speech will be good to other participants due to the proximity of the microphone to your mouth, you will avoid the "echo" effect. This is where participants hear themselves slightly delayed, due to the speakers on another person's computer getting picked up by the microphone. If you have ever experienced this, you will know how off-putting it is.

The advice I have given earlier about planning your session, slide use and content, all applies. A good set of slides for a live session is still a good set of slides for an online session. The differences are more due to the constraints of the virtual environment. You cannot usually see all of the audience, you may not be able to hear them all, you cannot guarantee what they are looking at, and you certainly cannot pick up on their body language. Indeed, they may have gone for a coffee break during your presentation, and you may not know about it!

I am therefore going to suggest some additional actions that should keep your audience engaged and interested, even if they are not in the same physical room. Unlike entering a real room, people may feel a stranger when entering a virtual room. If they have not attended an online session before, or if they have not used the meeting software that you are using before, they will have feelings of unease and unfamiliarity. Therefore, at the start of any online session, someone (often the host) should welcome participants, and then give a quick guide of the virtual meeting's interface. Attendees will want to know how to make themselves heard and how to give feedback. Most online meeting systems have some quick method for providing feedback from attendees, usually akin to setting a status. Attendees will want to know how to raise their virtual hand. Ensure that this familiarisation does not take too long, or become too much of a chore. After all, the important part is not the virtual environment.

At this stage, you should also verify that all the attendees can hear you. I often combine this with the guided tour of the interface, and ask attendees to put their virtual hand up, or set their status to "agree" if they are able to hear me. If someone cannot hear you, determining how long to wait for them to sort out their technical problems is not a precise science. I take the view that you should not wait too long. By all means provide some time for them to try to resolve their problem, but every minute that you wait is another minute when the other online attendees could be distracted by things happening in the place where they are. Particularly if attendees are in their own home, times when nothing is happening are times when they may think about other things, or be taken off task by other household members. You should also remember that if attendees are using a telephone for the meeting audio, their appearance in your virtual meeting room may not coincide with them having audio for the meeting. Do not assume that if they cannot hear straight away that there is a problem.

Of course, one way to minimise the likelihood of attendees having technical problems is to encourage them to test their set up beforehand. The better online meeting systems tend to have test pages that people can visit before the meeting, in order to ensure that their hardware will function without issues. This is something that you should include in the invitation emails to the session.

While I am dealing with audio, noise can be a problem in a way that it is not in a conventional presentation. In a normal presentation, if someone whispers, or rustles their papers, it is unlikely to distract the presenter (even if there is a minor distraction to attendees seated nearby). In the online environment, anything picked up by an attendee's microphone will be heard by everyone else at full volume, including those presenting. I would suggest that in the initial welcome and quick tour, you tell people how to mute their microphone using the online meeting software. Almost all software has this facility. In addition, the presenters and host usually have the ability to mute other people in the virtual meeting, with the attendees then unable to unmute themselves. This can be useful, as you as a presenter can then unmute a single person who has signalled that they have a question or some feedback, and then they can address the meeting. Since people cannot see each other, this type of management of who is speaking is more important than when face-to-face. However, you should ensure that everyone in the session knows how you will operate if you are planning to mute everyone by default. Simply muting everyone without explaining first may upset some people, as they may incorrectly assume that they will not be allowed to speak during the session.

When speaking in an online session, you may want to change slightly the style that you adopt. In a standard business presentation, a conversational style is often the most appropriate. You don't want to sound as if you are giving a sermon. However, in the online environment, you will need to slow your speech slightly from a normal speaking speed, and ensure that you are speaking clearly. You should also check that you are not inadvertently blowing or breathing directly into the microphone. Mumbling or unclear speech is harder for people to decipher if they can only hear audio. But like most of the advice in this book, don't go too far and speak too slowly. The overall aim is clarity rather than slowness.

At the start of an online presentation, a nervous attendee asked if I could see her. It turned out that she was worried that her webcam would be activated without her permission. I did reassure her that she would have to activate her webcam herself, but it did remind me that being seen in a virtual environment can be a tricky business. I take the view that as a presenter, you should be seen by those attending the meeting. That is a realistic expectation of the attendees; people like to know who is speaking to them. If you were in a conventional situation, everyone could see you. Therefore, in a virtual meeting I always switch on my webcam at the start. I feel that this gives a more personal and human touch when people are arriving. Of course, I make sure that I look fairly presentable; it is very easy to be inappropriately dressed when presenting from the comfort of your own home! I also make sure that as much as possible, there is not too much in view. This is not about distraction; it is more about giving a professional impression to the audience. Having minimal clutter in view gives a much more professional impression to those attending. However, I am not counting bookshelves as clutter, but things that look untidy. Remember that it is not a reality television show, but still a business presentation. In the same way that I would not deliver a face-to-face session wearing very casual clothes, I want to project a business-like atmosphere in an online meeting by having an appropriate webcam view. Having done introductions and perhaps even the overview with the webcam switched on, I sometimes then switch it off for the main presentation. This is only a personal preference, although it seems to be quite accepted as something to do. It is often more to do with being able to quickly check my notes or timings unnoticed. There is no reason not to have the webcam showing the presenter throughout the session.

It is a different situation when it comes to the audience. In a conventional presentation situation, the attendees are not "on show" in quite the same way as the presenter. Although they can be seen, the attention is focused on the person delivering the presentation. In an online setting, this should be the default for them. So having their webcam showing them all the time is likely to be uncomfortable, as the attention is being focused on them in a way that it would not be in a live situation. A presentation has a different dynamic to a business meeting, where all attendees can expect to be the focus at points throughout the meeting session. In a presentation, they have a reasonable expectation not to be. Therefore, in a presentation situation, regular attendees should not have to display themselves on a webcam, in my opinion.

The online setting can present some challenges for dealing with queries. Since your attendees cannot catch your eye in the way that they could in a face-to-face setting, they may find it helpful to have a protocol to follow for questions and queries. Some online environments have a special part of them for questions and answers. As you (or another person with moderator/presenter permissions) respond to queries, all participants can see the questions and answers, forming a dynamic FAQ bank. In most online environments, this is not the case. However, they all tend to have a text chat facility. My suggestion would be that attendees type their queries into the chat, and then at points during the presentation you can go through them and answer them verbally. If you try to answer them by typing, and also present at the same time, it would be very difficult to achieve both to a good standard simultaneously. In my earlier chapters, I mentioned that having explicit pauses for questions is often a good idea. In an online setting, I think it is essential. Having a moment where there is an expectation of input from the audience can help prevent their experience being too passive. You may also need to pause for longer than you would in a live situation, as attendees may need to locate their microphone or spend time typing in the text chat area.

While you might think that an online presentation is going to impose limitations of what can be done, there is one area where you may have more possibilities. Most online meeting environments have some form of voting or polling. In face-to-face meetings, this can be cumbersome and potentially complex to set up with audience response systems, but in online meetings it is usually an integral part of the software. Using the voting feature could form part of an engaging starter activity, or useful for seeing what your audience already knows about the topic of the presentation. Of course, you can also use the feedback for simple yes/no voting, as long as your attendees don't mind their responses being public. Asking your audience whether they would like you to go into a little more detail on part of the content will help to keep them engaged.

The other aspect of managing a presentation that is easier online is presenting slides in a non-linear way. Most online environments allow the presenter to see thumbnail images of all the slides. In this way, you can select any slide in your presentation and move on from there. While the same is true for a live presentation, your audience will often see what you are doing if your computer's display in projected onto the main screen. Online, your audience need never know that they are not seeing the slides in the original order in which they appear in the presentation. It is also therefore much easier to have slides that you keep in reserve, in case the attendees show an interest in a particular section.

While presenting online brings its own challenges, it is increasingly an environment where the business presenter will need to feel comfortable. To put your mind at ease and feel relaxed, practise first and ensure that the technology works as it should.

Epilogue

So after making it this far, you should have plenty of ideas to make your presentations engaging, and engaging presentations are usually effective presentations. If I had to sum up the main messages that will serve you well in any business presentation situation that you might find yourself in, then they would be these.

Understand your audience and what their expectations are. Manage their expectations at the start and throughout.

The difference between a good presentation and an average one is the presenter. The technology is there to support you, but not to take over.

Keep plenty of variety in the learning styles, slide types and speaking; remember that every technique is most effective when used in moderation.

If you want to take your professional development of presenting skills in a business environment further, there are plenty of people who you can contact who will be able to help you. My advice would be to find people who have experience of the business environment and who also understand about how people learn and process information. There is a lot written about presentation skills that I don't particularly agree with, and I have seen some particularly dodgy things on the web. It is not an act that you are putting on, and in some ways, the audience are buying into you as a person, with all your skills and experience, as you engage them.

I wish you well, and hope that as you try some of the things that I have put in this book, they work well for you. Go and surprise your audience, in a good way!

Appendix A – Displaying video

Showing some video in a presentation can add to engagement, but often it causes a disproportionate number of problems.

The first thing to check is that the computer that will be displaying the video is able to successfully play back the file format that the video clip uses. To do this, it must have the correct codec installed, which is software to decode the file. It can be dangerous to assume that all machines have the right codecs installed, which is why you may wish to use your own laptop if you are using video clips.

Sometimes, when using a laptop or computer with multiple display outputs, video displays on only one of the displays. This is typical on older machines. If this happens, then the video usually is shown on the primary display adapter. If that does not happen to be the display that your audience can see, then go into the properties of your computer's display adapter and choose to make the appropriate output the primary output.

If you wish to have a slide that will start showing a video clip in full screen mode when displayed, then that is fairly straightforward to achieve and looks good to the audience. You can of course simply resize the video on the slide so that it fills it. If the video is of a different aspect ratio than the slide, then you can set the background of the slide to black. In the Keynote® presentation application, the default is to start playing the movie clip automatically. This can be changed by selecting the clip on the slide, and opening the Inspector pane. You will then see the properties for the movie clip, although you may have to select the appropriate option on the top of the pane. For the PowerPoint® presentation application, once the video has been inserted onto a slide you will be prompted to choose whether to start playing automatically. Otherwise, access the properties for the video clip. This is done by clicking on the clip on the slide to select it, and then choosing the "Playback" ribbon that will display once the clip is selected. You can then use the ribbon to select to play in full screen and to start automatically rather than when clicked. Save the presentation when done.

Appendix B – PowerPoint® keyboard shortcuts

Using quick keyboard shortcuts can help you appear more polished in your presentation style to the audience. Also, they will not see any menus appear that detract from the slides' messages. There are many shortcuts that you can use as you edit your presentation. The ones below are those that are useful when presenting in front of an audience.

This is not intended as an exhaustive list; rather a set of recommendations of keyboard shortcuts that you will find useful.

Key press	Effect
F5	Starts the presentation
Shift-F5	Starts the presentation at the currently selected slide.
N	Next slide
Enter Spacebar Right arrow	Next slide or animation
P	Previous slide
B	Show a completely black screen
W	Show a completely white screen
Ctrl-H	Hide the arrow pointer
Ctrl-A	Show the arrow pointer
x+Enter	Go to the slide number x, e.g. 12+Enter goes to slide 12.

These shortcuts have been tested with PowerPoint® 2010 but may also work on previous versions.

Appendix C – Keynote® keyboard shortcuts

If you are a user of Keynote®, then you can also use keyboard shortcuts to provide a more polished presentation style for the audience. As with the previous Appendix, I have included the most useful ones when running the presentation with an audience. There are many others that you may find useful when designing the presentation, which are referenced on Apple's web site.

This is not intended as an exhaustive list; rather a set of recommendations of keyboard shortcuts that you will find useful.

Key press	Effect
Option – Command-P	Starts the presentation
Right square bracket "]"	Next slide
N, Spacebar, Return, Page Down, Right Arrow	Next slide or animation
"Home" key	Go to first slide
"End" key	Go to last slide
P	Previous slide
B	Show a completely black screen
W	Show a completely white screen
C	Hide or show the arrow pointer
x+Enter	Go to the slide number x in theslide switcher, e.g. 12+Enter goes to slide 12.

These shortcuts have been tested with Keynote® 09 but may also work on other versions.

Acknowledgements

Microsoft Office and PowerPoint are trademarks of Microsoft Corporation in the United States and/or other countries.

Keynote is a trademark of Apple Inc., registered in the US and other countries.

Prezi is a trademark of Prezi Inc.

Twitter and Tweet are trademarks of Twitter, Inc. in the United States and other countries.

Every effort has been made to use and acknowledge trademarks in accordance with the trademark holder's guidelines. If you consider that your intellectual property has been used or acknowledged inappropriately, I would appreciate the opportunity to put that right. In such a situation, please contact the author.

Works Cited

Felder, R. M., & Silverman, L. K. (1998). *Learning and Teaching Styles.* Engineering Education.

Contact the author

If you would like to make contact with the author about any aspect of this work, email him at richard@businesspresentationtraining.co.uk.